T0243345

Reclaiming Venus

The Many Lives of Alvenia Bridges

Alvenia Bridges & Maya Angela Smith

RISING ACTION

ISBN: 978-1-998076-70-3
Ebook: 978-1-998076-72-7

BIO005000 BIOGRAPHY & AUTOBIOGRAPHY / Entertainment & Performing Arts
BIO004000 BIOGRAPHY & AUTOBIOGRAPHY / Music
BIO002010 BIOGRAPHY & AUTOBIOGRAPHY / Cultural, Ethnic & Regional / African & Black

#ReclaimingVenus

Contents

This book is dedicated to James Finney, who took Alvenia to the highest plane with his plaits, and to Roberta Flack, who saw how the world means everything to everyone.

This memoir is the author's story. The memories and experiences are from her recollection and may not reflect the experiences of those featured in the book. Alvenia looks back on her life in the music industry with fondness, love, and gratitude.

Reclaiming Venus

Prologue

Fig 1. Alvenia in her breakfast nook. By Maya Angela Smith.

Fig 2. Alvenia in her office. By Maya Angela Smith.

I entered the black, metal-framed, double doors of the building at the corner of 58th Street and 7th Avenue. Stepping over the threshold provided some relief from the muggy New York summer air and the bustling of clueless tourists that had descended on the city. I had no luggage with me other than a backpack because my suitcase never made it on the plane. A baggage handlers' strike at Charles de Gaulle airport in Paris ensured that I would be without my possessions for at least a week, leaving me even grumpier than usual after a transatlantic flight. I approached the doorman and stated my business—trying to sound official since I had never really interacted with doormen before. They were characters in movies set in upper-class New York City. I never expected that I would be living in a building that required them.

Florian, the doorman in question, greeted me with a smile. "Miss Alvenia has been expecting you. The elevator is over there. You may proceed to the eighth floor."

Over a decade earlier, I had called New York City home. As a college student on a scholarship, the only apartments I had ever lived in were five-story walkups. Somehow, I had found a room in this fancy building and yet I was paying a fraction of what I did in the early 2000s. Alvenia described the space that I would be subletting from her as an adorable little room with an ensuite bath. For $800 a month and only a block from Central Park, I was pretty sure I would be sleeping on a mat next to the toilet and using the sink to shield my face from falling paint chips. Finding a room like the one she described, in a prime location for such a low price seemed too good to be true.

As I knocked, the door swung open. She must have been informed of my arrival because she was waiting for me with a huge grin. As I entered what would be my home for the next three months, I was immediately struck by how regal this woman was. She was statuesque—her six-foot frame towered over me, even though her back was slightly bowed. She wore a simple strand of pearls around her neck, accentuated by the smoothness of her brown skin and the ripples of her black flowing outfit. Her eyes, meanwhile, conveyed the accumulation of wisdom that comes from a lifetime of experiences. As I studied her face, Alvenia's warm voice resonated in the hallway, "You must be Maya. Please, come in. Welcome to your new home."

She gave me a tour of the apartment, starting with the kitchen and breakfast nook, then my room, which was adjacent to the kitchen, followed by a large living room that was partitioned with a silk accordion screen. The right side of the partition was fashioned as a hybrid library and art gallery, with grand, overflowing bookcases and large-format oil paintings leaning against empty wall space. Her bed was in the corner on the left side of the partition, along with a desk, a sofa, and a table. She then pointed out a spacious, sunny bedroom at the end of the long hall, which our other roommate occupied and the bathroom that they shared. I couldn't get over the height of the ceilings and the detail in the crown molding.

"You must be tired, dear. Why don't you go rest?"

I took Alvenia up on her offer. Although I had so many questions, they could wait. I hadn't gotten a good look at my room yet and even after witnessing the opulence of the rest of the space, I wanted to inspect where I would be sleeping for the summer. The room was a perfect size for me and while the bathroom was cramped, it offered everything I needed. I was still confused about how much real estate I got for only $800 a month. But at that moment, the overwhelming emotion I felt was delight. My living arrangements were a nice antidote to the chaos of my trip.

When I groggily emerged from my room a couple of hours later, Alvenia met me in the kitchen. "Would you like some tea?" she inquired.

"Herbal, if you have it, please."

"That's all I have." Upon hearing that, I realized that we would get along. She then motioned for me to sit at the little round table in the kitchen while she prepared our tea.

I knew very little of my new roommate other than some scant background information from the mutual friend who had put us in touch. This friend was someone I hadn't spoken to in years, but who had happened upon my plea for housing in New York on Facebook. There is always anticipation when encountering a new roommate, but my introductory phone call with Alvenia had left me with a sense of immense excitement. When I hung up with her, a voice in my head told me that meeting her would be a life-changing experience.

While waiting for our tea to steep, I admired all the photos pinned on the wall above the table. The breakfast nook was plastered with incredible images, many adorned with beautiful inscriptions: photos of Bob Marley signed by his favorite photographer, Kate Simon; portraits of Roberta Flack and Dizzy Gillespie with heartfelt notes scribbled in their handwriting; a blown-up copy of a color polaroid of Jimi Hendrix strumming his red guitar outside his home in Seattle when he was just a boy. This image was juxtaposed with a black-and-white photo of Jimi waiting on a bench in an airport, taken shortly before his death. Someone had drawn angel wings on his back with sharpie. I then noticed a black-and-white photo of a much younger Alvenia modeling a stunning dress, as she presented the viewer with her profile. The kaleidoscope of images went on and on, consuming all blank space.

"If you think that's impressive, you should see my office." She winked. She then grabbed her mug and beckoned me to follow.

It was true. The objects hanging in the breakfast nook were only the tip of the iceberg. She proudly drew my attention to even more impressive memorabilia suspended above her office desk: two framed records encased in glass—identical except that one was gold and the other platinum—with her name engraved next to an image of Mick Jagger's first solo album cover "She's the Boss"; a black-and-white photo of Mick during the height of his Rolling Stones' career; a color photo of Mick huddled together with other rock and roll legends—Tina Turner,

Madonna, Bob Dylan ... the list went on. A black-and-white photo of Alvenia and a man I didn't recognize rounded out the series. The two of them were looking at each other with such respect and admiration. The inscription read, "Don't ever forget—don't *ever* forget how good you are ... —Bill."

I asked Alvenia about these objects that she so lovingly displayed and each one catapulted her into sharing a distant memory. At first, I didn't know what to expect, but as she casually said things like, "Oh that's when I was working on *Live Aid*," or "That's when I was Mick's personal business liaison," or "Roberta was how I got into the music business," or "I was with Jimi the days leading up to his passing,"

I would have to stop her and say, "Wait, what?"

She would always laugh. "Those were from another life. Another time. I'll tell you the stories behind them someday soon."

The next day, I set off to begin the project that had brought me to New York in the first place. I was conducting qualitative fieldwork for a book on language and identity in the Senegalese diaspora. I planned to spend the summer interviewing members of the Senegalese community all over the city to add to research already collected in Paris and Rome. For the next three months, I navigated the city, visiting the West African markets up in Harlem and the cultural centers down in Brooklyn, attending Senegalese dance classes in the Bronx and luncheons in Queens, all the while capturing the experiences of those I interacted with through interviews. I came home each night exhausted by the hours on my feet but also excited because my day of gathering stories would have only just begun. My evenings became my opportunity to learn Alvenia's story and the multiple worlds that she once inhabited.

The first evening of storytelling—all our storytelling sessions would only commence once tea was served—consisted of my staring wide-eyed at her as she began to pull back the wrapping on her former life. Once I got over my initial shock, I fumbled into my pocket and pulled out the digital recorder that I used to interview people. I then stopped Alvenia mid-sentence, "Alvenia, would you mind if I recorded you? I could email you the files so you would always have a record."

"Of course you may record me, but I don't really know anything about email. I sort of lost interest in new technology once I stopped working in the music industry. I can barely work voicemail on my phone."

"That's okay. I'll show you how to access them if you ever need to."

She then continued with the first story she shared with me—pointing to a photo and explaining why she was dressed so impeccably in white surrounded by a sea of people also shrouded in white. The photo was taken in the eighties, decades before *dîner en blanc* parties became a global trend. "This was from Ashford and Simpson's annual Fourth of July white party," she continued. "I looked forward to these gatherings every year."

As 1:00 a.m. rolled around, I thanked Alvenia for sharing so much of her life with me but informed her that I must go to sleep. I often wondered if she ever slept.

I asked if we could continue the conversation the following day and she responded, "Of course, darling. I would be happy to tell you more about my life if you're interested."

I assured her that I would love that and then retired to my room.

We got into the lovely habit of meeting in the evening over tea and tales. We exchanged stories of our lives. I was always amazed at how riveted she was by my own stories, considering that she had lived the lives of what seemed like many different people, each one more wondrous than the last. As we sank into this familiarity, she started sharing with me all of her story—not just the glitzy and glamorous insights into being a model in Europe or the absurd behind-the-scenes chaos of working with some of the biggest musical acts in the world, but also about her troubled childhood against the backdrop of societal rot and the moment that she fell down to the earth after soaring so high. I accompanied her on this journey, feeling immense joy, inspiration, anger and sadness as she wove tales of despair and rejection with those of success and triumph. I kept thinking to myself how fortunate the world would be if they ever got to hear her voice. She had spent a lot of her life behind the scenes. What if she could finally have a stage of her own?

A few days before I was set to leave New York, Alvenia turned to me after sharing a particularly emotional memory. "You know, it has been my dream to write my memoir. Numerous people have told me that I should. On several occasions I've tried, but each time, life would get in the way or people tasked with writing my story would fail to see the true essence of what I am about. After spending these months rehashing the experiences of my life, I finally want to try again. Would you help me?"

I was taken aback by her request at first. She had shared parts of her life story with so many people. I mean, how could people not inquire about her life when they saw her walls meticulously adorned with the relics of an almost fantastical past? Why was she entrusting me with bringing her words and her wisdom to a larger audience?

I pondered our generational gap. I am four decades her junior. She lived many of her most dramatic experiences before I was even born. The musical acts she supported during her decade in the music industry did not even cross my radar until long after these performers had exited their prime. Yet, Alvenia and I resonated with each other in a way where the age difference quickly dissipated whenever we were locked in dialogue.

We share a variegated perspective on understanding what it is like being highly mobile Black women who have travelled the world and have experienced the ebb and flow of life in motion. I have arguably had a much easier experience in reaching the far corners of the globe. As a child of the eighties, I had more of a leg up than Alvenia ever had. I am the product of two people who came of age in the volatile sixties, who attended segregated schools in the South and who, because of relentless warriors who fought and demanded equal rights, went to prestigious colleges against the backdrop of Vietnam War activism, as well as the Black Power and Women's Liberation movements. I grew up in the wake of my parents' and ancestors' sacrifices, which gave me a more expansive understanding of what I should demand for myself and how I should conceptualize my own humanity. Their struggles and accomplishments also paved the way for me to access what my ancestors could only dream of. I could earn a PhD, become a professor, and travel to and live in multiple countries. While the number of Black women professors in the country is dismal, at least I am not the first. I, thus, have a very particular relationship to notions of race and gender, as well as to the places where I have lived and visited, both in America and throughout the world.

Alvenia, by virtue of her upbringing and the timing of her birth, encountered this world in a very different way. She was an unwitting player in the desegregation of America and her personal experience serves to illustrate the human trauma associated with demanding liberation and equality. By the 1950s, the country may have slowly been moving toward justice, but little children like Alvenia were often forced to bear the scars of an unjust world. I thought that I knew what this experience was like from hearing about my parents' experiences under Jim Crow and reading personal accounts from the period. But it wasn't until I heard Alvenia's story—of failing to integrate a public school and how the repercussions of this reverberated in various ways throughout her life—did I realize that this formative experience would dictate how Alvenia learned to engage with the world and color how she would approach interactions around race for a lifetime. But while I am hyperaware of how being a Black woman influences my lived experiences, Alvenia has been less concerned with the restrictions that the world has tried to place on her, instead focusing on simply being who she knows how to be: Alvenia.

I have experienced nowhere near the same amount of racist vitriol that she has encountered in her lifetime, nor have I been subjected to the extent of lowered expectations that she endured during her childhood and working career, when everyone around her assumed failure based on her race or her gender. Yet, many of the emotions she conveyed to me and disappointments that she had to overcome were ones I've wrestled with as well. The world has always been very adept at creating scripts based on preset conditions and shoehorning people into stereotypes that limit their potential and their worth. While the world has evolved a lot since Alvenia's arrival on this planet, in many ways it has stayed the same. Alvenia's story is just as relevant today as it was when her story began to form.

In many ways, her life is testament to what can be achieved when one faces adversity head on. Alvenia transformed failure into the fuel that allowed her to take the world on in her own creative way. The successes that she was able to cobble together against the odds convey her indomitable spirit and the stories that she tells from her time in the music and fashion industries would impress anyone. But for me, their true value is in how she navigated these spaces that were not meant for her, as a woman, a Black person, or both. Unfortunately, her trailblazing somehow got left out of the history books. As I stood in awe of her ability to live her life fully, authentically and on her terms—when she was never supposed to—I realized that most people have never gotten past the razzle-dazzle that she has chosen to display through the carefully curated artifacts on her wall. Her life means so much more than the sum of its parts.

Ruminating on her request, I was overcome with a tremendous sense of purpose. It was as if she and I had been transmitting on the same wavelength our whole lives but only now were we simultaneously tuning into the same frequency. I reminded myself that I had dedicated my life to creating a platform to amplify those voices that would normally go unheard. Converting people's stories to written form had become my calling and I was now being gifted with the most extraordinary life story that I had ever encountered. I started to understand that it was through our friendship, through the joy that we cultivated in our storytelling sessions and through my faith in the power of listening, that a fuller picture of Alvenia Bridges had emerged. I told her that writing her story would be my greatest honor.

While teeming with excitement, I began to feel overwhelmed by this monumental task. The diversity and disparity of experiences that Alvenia had shared with me over a few months indicated that I was not telling the singular life of a woman. I needed to find a way to do justice to her many lives, because Alvenia was a master of reinventing herself.

She smiled at me with her watchful eyes while peering over the metallic rim of her teacup, the wall of photographs perfectly framing her regal posture. As my gaze darted from the autographed photographs of musical legends pinned overhead, to Alvenia's black-and-white modeling photos, I soon understood that these artifacts were the key. Our storytelling sessions almost always started off with her sharing a piece of memorabilia that would teleport her back to a past life and purpose.

Because of my training as an ethnographer, my goal has always been to study people's lives and their relationships to their communities by applying a cultural lens. Artifacts and the ways in which people interact with them, provide illuminating insight about how we make meaning in the world. They also convey intimate knowledge about particular cultural moments. Alvenia has witnessed and been a driving force in some of the largest cultural moments of the 20th century, moments that span both time and space. Meanwhile, Alvenia's ability to move throughout the world, from Kansas City to Los Angeles, New York, Geneva, Portofino, London, Paris, Sydney, and beyond, after having grown up in a town that would not even let her move within the white-only sections, highlights the importance of mobility in her narrative.

Therefore, the best way to unravel Alvenia's story is by highlighting her relationships to people, places, and things. This book chronicles Alvenia's whirlwind journey through a focus on the global places that she has occupied and the extraordinary people who she has touched. However, at the same time, her apartment and the memories contained in the photos and memorabilia that decorate her walls keep her grounded in the present, while allowing her to return to her illustrious past. Because of their centrality to her life, these treasures serve as the lynchpin to her narrative. The following pages thus represent the life and times of Alvenia Bridges—her stories intertwined with my experiences of getting to know her, as well as the objects she holds dear in her New York City apartment, the first and only place that she has truly called home.

Part 1: Dreaming of the World

CHAPTER ONE

The Long Escape from Kansas

"Baby girl, tell me what's the matter," my grandma, who I affectionately called Mama, pleaded as I buried my young adolescent head in her lap to hide the tears. She gently stroked my hair. She had been dutifully massaging grease into my scalp and taking the pointed end of the comb to create parts for my four braids, but at this moment, she paused to tend to my emotional wounds. My sporadic visits to Mama's house, across the border in Missouri, were the highlights of my childhood. When the pressures of dysfunctional family life and society's racial vitriol became too much for me to bear, I would set out from my small Kansas town to the one refuge that I had in the world.

Mama was the only person who ever seemed to want me around. My mother, Zonnetta, wasn't an unpleasant person, she was actually well respected in the community. She had flawless taste and loved to sew, so she would make beautiful dresses for my sisters and I to wear for Easter and other special occasions. I was always very presentable, but I also knew that Zonnetta wasn't interested in having me as a daughter. She didn't know how to be a mother and never bothered trying to learn. My stepfather, Ed Madden, on the other hand, was a flat-out unfriendly human being. While Zonnetta was devoid of any motherly instincts, Ed Madden was the antithesis of fatherly. When I was nine years old, I started sleeping with a knife under my pillow because there was something about him that I didn't trust, even though at the time there was nothing specific that drove me to take such a drastic measure, except the underdeveloped but intuitive reasoning of a young child. He seemed like trouble, so I spent my childhood trying to avoid him at all costs. In fact, I tended to avoid most people. The fewer people I let into my heart, the less disappointment I would face.

The fact that I was a loner made it easier to deal with my younger sisters, who were a tightknit group who never really accepted me as theirs. Perhaps it was because I had a different father than they did, or perhaps it was because they were into different things than I was. The reasons didn't matter. I vowed to love them despite how they treated me. I saw myself as their protector, because living in our house was hard on everyone. So, when they would scatter like flies as soon as Zonnetta left for work in the morning, I would make sure that the house was spotless upon her return, even if I had to do the chores that were meant for all of us by myself. Mother didn't care *how* they were done, as long as they *were* done.

Besides, many things were much easier since my family moved to the house on Cleveland Avenue in Kansas City in the mid-1950s. Before this house in town, we had lived on a farm. There, when my sisters would disappear, I alone would have to kill, pluck, and cook one of our chickens for supper. Even though I was duty-bound, imposing death on a living creature had never come easy to me. The business of killing chickens was even dirtier in my mind because it was the only useful thing Ed Madden ever taught me—along with the capacity that men had for violence. Fortunately, I no longer had to kill chickens once we moved to town. I contented myself with that one improvement in life.

But I exchanged killing chickens for the slow death that your spirit suffers when subjected to unending racial hatred. Our new house in town was indeed nicer. Our yard even had a large tree that I loved climbing in my spare time and resorted to hiding in when I needed an escape. But this shiny, new house belied the dark underbelly of a state and a nation in turmoil. The 1954 Supreme Court decision on *Brown vs the Board of Education* had roiled Kansas. We lived only fifty miles east of Topeka, the epicenter of a massive struggle to end school segregation. While racial segregation was deemed unconstitutional, it would take almost two decades before the stalwarts in the farthest reaches of the country gave in to a progression towards equality.

Our new house was in an all-white neighborhood and the KKK had made sure to welcome us with their usual brand of hospitality. Black families throughout the South were no strangers to rocks through windows and racial epithets that seemed to linger in the air long after screeching tires carried away their owners in the dead of night. Even so, we never got used to the violence inflicted on us, such as when faceless neighbors set our pickup truck on fire. Ed Madden had taken it out on us extra hard that night, seeming to absorb the anger and hate that the white folks harbored for us simply for the color of our skin and transforming it into an aggression meant for the only people he had power over—his family. I doubt this displaced rage actually soothed his soul, but it did strengthen my resolve to escape Kansas and all its transgressions.

"I failed my mother," I hiccupped between sobs, head still buried in Mama's skirt. I had finally steadied myself to answer Mama's question, quieted by the care that she was showing for my hair.

"Honey," she looked down with those solemn eyes, "you did what any strong girl would've done in that circumstance. You can't be too hard on yourself."

I was still wearing my best Sunday outfit—the only clothes Zonnetta said would be presentable enough in court, since I had ruined my white dress. She had barely spoken to me since the incident, other than to repeat how I was a failure. Zonnetta didn't accept any backtalk. I just had to swallow my imagined retorts and block out the surge of pain that jolted my heart each time she cursed my name.

An all-white neighborhood meant an all-white school, so I had been bussed to a predominantly Black school miles away ever since the move. The PTA of that school had chosen me, along with a couple of other Black students, to integrate the all-white neighborhood school. I was a good student who loved to learn and I worked with the librarian, so the PTA agreed I should be included in the group of integrators. Zonnetta, who was on the PTA, had doubts about whether I could pull off this assignment or not because I was not known for sitting back and allowing bullies to pick on those weaker than they were. Once, when my baby brother Robert failed to return home from the grocery store, I had found some older bullies beating him up. I'd flung my body between him and them. It was admittedly not very ladylike.

"The Lord is my shepherd, I shall not want," stumbled off my tongue as I marched toward the school door that first day. I had proven to Zonnetta that I knew the whole verse by heart, because her explicit instructions to me were to say it over and over in case there was trouble.

Under no circumstance was I to even think a violent thought. They told us there would be police. There were. While I learned from a young age that the police weren't there to protect me, I was still shocked by the way those officers looked at us with the same derision as the jeering onlookers who yelled and spat in our faces. I was wearing the white dress Zonnetta had made for the occasion. I had matching white socks and white shoes. I was pristine and defiant, gaining courage as I walked along the wall toward the school's main entrance. Suddenly, glass Coke bottles began to fly around me, shards ricocheting as they shattered against the pavement. I looked down to find blood on my socks. Was it mine? I had asked Zonnetta why they hated me because of my skin, but she never explained why. She did nothing more than to act as if she hadn't heard me.

As the shrapnel of exploded bottles burst around me, I caught sight of one of the white boys who was throwing those bottles. I grabbed him so quickly that I will never forget the look of surprise on his face. I dragged him down and put my knee on his throat. I was about to raise my fist when a burly policeman grabbed me by my neck and shoulders and pinned me down. While he straddled my body to cuff me, his eyes bored a hole into my face. Those piercing eyes were brimming with the hatred that I had endured my whole life. The racial animus, so indicative of my surroundings, clung to the air and stagnated as the onlookers cheered my detention.

I had promised no violence. I had broken that promise. So, I ended up in juvenile court. Just me. No one else was punished. The white protesters with their broken bottles—jagged edges scraping away my humanity—went on with their daily lives. I sat there in the courtroom, sat there drowning in Zonnetta's humiliation as they read off my punishment. She didn't speak to me all day. When we got home, I asked if I could help her with the chores, but she simply shook her head. Even though she never said a kind word to me, I still yearned for her love and tried to do everything I could to make up for whatever it was that kept her from loving me. I went to the backyard and climbed up my favorite tree. I went up there to seek forgiveness and decided that I would try to never care about the color of my skin ever again. I asked God to rid me of what I called racial karma—a fate that I didn't understand but which followed me around for some unknown reason. I then became bolder in my supplications and asked to be rid of Kansas. I worried though, that God had stopped listening to me years ago.

I felt so alone, so isolated. The disappointment Zonnetta had worn on her face that day made her lack of love all the more palpable. I began shivering with anger, but that anger soon dissolved into sadness. I was becoming despondent, but then, out of nowhere, I started hearing a quiet voice in my head telling me that I already had what I needed. That voice had never made itself known to me before. Who was speaking to me? I briefly thought that perhaps I was going crazy, but the voice had such a calming influence. It didn't tell me that everything would be okay. It simply beseeched me to believe in myself. This was the first time that this essence, which I would one day call the Spirit, decided to visit me.

The quiet voice helped me realize that at that moment, what I needed most was the contact of someone who loved me for me. I climbed down from my tree sanctuary and set out for my grandma's house.

After what seemed like hours of silence, as Mama Beatrice washed, oiled, and braided my hair, she looked up at me and said, "Baby, if you could have anything in the world, what would it be?" No one had ever posed that question to me before. In fact, I had never allowed myself to dream before. How can you dream when you are so focused on surviving each moment? How can you dream when life is a waking nightmare? Biting my lip in deep concentration, I pondered her question for a moment and then, straightening my back, I looked up at Mama with a newfound sense of calm.

With no inflection in my voice, I finally spoke aloud the dream that had been lying dormant deep inside for all those years, "I want to leave Kansas, Mama. I want to see the world. If I don't leave, I'll either be dead or in jail."

Mama gently patted me on the head and nodded.

A few weeks later, when I visited Mama again, she pulled out a package wrapped in delicate cloth. She smiled. "Honey, I want you to make me one promise. I want you to finish school. Just finish high school, baby and I'll get you out." She then handed over the mystery package. As I unwrapped the twine and pulled back the cloth, a gorgeous globe emerged. It was my first globe. She whispered, "This represents my oath to you. If you finish high school, you will be able to go anywhere that you can find on this globe." This was one promise that I could keep. True to her word, Mama would eventually keep her end of the bargain and facilitate my escape from Kansas.

In the meantime, I had to somehow get through several more years of humiliation and exclusion. Although integrating into the all-white school hadn't worked out, I saw a silver lining in my failure; I didn't really want to be subjected to the same taunts and disdain at school that I received simply for walking in my neighborhood. As such, things got a little better when I started attending the Catholic high school, Bishop Ward. For one, they had integrated in 1945, a decade before all public schools were mandated to do so. At the time, Kansas was in a curious position when it came to rolling out integration. Of the five states arguing before the Supreme Court in the early fifties to safeguard racial segregation in public schools (including South Carolina, Virginia, Delaware, and the District of Columbia), Kansas had historically taken a more multifaceted approach. Segregation was not codified in state law and in fact, all state colleges, as well as most high schools and junior highs, were already integrated. My town of Kansas City was the only place in the state where public high schools were racially segregated because, as a border town, it followed the lead of its Missouri neighbor. Bishop Ward touted its devotion to giving all people of God access to a Christian education and used this reasoning to convince its parishioners to integrate. While many families had withdrawn their children, the school community survived integration.[1]

However, just because I was allowed to be there didn't mean that I truly belonged. I was an awkward kid with arms as inexplicably long as my legs and with nothing in between. My sisters were all given ample backsides. It was as if God had used up all of my flesh on my wiry limbs and decided to forego endowing me with anything more than a flat surface for a rump and a little stump for a torso. Zonnetta used to joke that if I sat on a quarter, ten cents would stick out. That was when she was being kind. She usually just shouted her preferred name for me, Orangutan, when she wanted me to acknowledge her. Looking so different from all my sisters was a constant reminder of how I didn't share their daddy. I blamed my lack of booty on whoever my father was. He had also bequeathed me my unusual nose. I had never met him. The only

---

1. To understand segregation in Kansas, see "Why Kansas?"

information Zonnetta shared with me was that he was part Blackfoot Indian.

Luckily, I was able to find solace in the world of books and spent my free periods sitting amongst the stacks reading anything that talked about foreign lands and different customs. I would then mark these places on my globe when I got home and think about how I would one day visit them. School signified my escape route. Mama knew that if I was educated, I could eventually go anywhere. She gave me that globe for encouragement and to remind me that I had to create dreams in order for them to ever become true. Besides, school was a much safer place than home, so I ended up spending a lot of my time there.

At least my love of learning offered a refuge. I couldn't say the same thing for my brother Robert, who was born a few years after me. School was a constant battle. Zonnetta and Ed Madden called him stupid when in reality, he was simply dyslexic. Because words didn't make sense in written form, it took him forever to learn how to write. But I knew that he was an incredible little boy. I would tell him about the people and places I learned about in my library books and he would ask the most inquisitive questions. I could see that he knew more about the world than most people his age. He grew up to prove me right eventually, but I wish I could've had this knowledge when we were children. It would've kept my heart from breaking as I watched him suffer at the hands of an abusive father and an uncaring world.

I tried to lessen the burden for each of my siblings the best way I knew how. Each afternoon, I would return from school and begin preparing dinner. I would then help them with their homework while tending to the stove. Zonnetta worked on Saturdays as well, so I would watch everyone while completing my chores. One particular Saturday afternoon, one of my sisters was sullener that usual. Several weeks before, it had crossed my mind that she always seemed to be in an exceptionally foul mood on Saturdays, but I had pushed the thought out of my head. Who knows what goes through the mind of a pre-adolescent girl? The following Sunday, I noticed a bruise on her arm that escaped the cover of her shirt sleeve, so I decided to investigate. Something told me that I should tread carefully.

We had never been close, so it was difficult to get my sister to open up to me at first. She had always been into the more typical girl things. She liked dolls and dresses and couldn't understand my penchant for getting into fights with the neighborhood bullies. Perhaps my reputation as a fighter was what finally convinced her to tell me, but my suspicions, the same ones that drove me to begin sleeping with a knife several years ago, didn't prepare me for the impact of hearing it aloud. While refusing to go into too much detail, she allowed me to share her secret about Ed Madden's Saturday visits, when he would touch her in a way that she knew was wrong. She was just a little girl, powerless in so many ways. Yet, she was strong enough to ask for help the only way she knew: by confiding in me. The shock that I felt quickly turned into an overwhelming sense of responsibility. I needed to make things right.

I resolved to talk to Zonnetta after church. I was hoping that the word of God would open her heart to what I had to say. When I approached her as she tended her garden, she seemed annoyed by my very presence. To muster courage, I repeated under my breath over and over that I was a fighter and needed to do this to deserve being called one. I instinctively waited until she had set the pruning shears down. Compared to how she was with her children, she was so gentle with the plants, gingerly patting the soil and whispering to the chrysanthemums that were just starting to bloom.

I knew never to interrupt her and didn't say a word until Zonnetta was ready to speak to me. While she didn't care much about me, she did manage to teach me a thing or two. For instance, she always put me in charge of the root vegetables in order to illustrate patience. She had to remind me on occasion that if you don't dig around enough to loosen the earth, you only pull up the carrot tops, which won't feed you. We relied on our garden vegetables for nourishment, so over the years, I had learned something about patience.

"Don't you have chores to do? Stop that stalling and spit it out so you can get back to your work," she said. She didn't even bother looking at me in administering this reproach.

I sucked in my breath and upon exhaling, I managed to tell her everything that my sister had said before having to draw another breath.

She calmly rose from her knees, took off her gloves, and motioned for me to come closer. Then, before I could register what was happening, she took the backside of her hand and smacked it across my face—each knuckle burrowing into the fleshy part of my cheeks for a split second and bouncing back on a wave of energy. She then took one of the weeds she had just pulled up and fashioned it into a switch. She proceeded to rap the length of my lanky arms repeatedly as I screamed for her to stop.

"Don't make a scene. You've already brought enough shame on us. Don't you dare make the neighbors think that I can't raise my children right. I will beat those lies out of your mouth, so help me God."

I didn't want to draw attention to our family, but I couldn't stand getting a whooping just for telling the truth. I decided to make a run for it, twisting myself out of her grasp and bolting into the house. I could feel the heat rising in the pit of my stomach before tamping it down as best I could. If I submitted to anger, I would become dangerous and there would be no stopping me. If I got myself thrown out of the house, there would be no way to offer the little protection that I could to my siblings. If I was thrown out, I knew I wouldn't be able to finish school. I was scrappy, but I couldn't imagine surviving on the streets. Would Mama take me in? She was always kept at arm's length, even when she wanted to help. I couldn't risk it. The tears that rolled down my face were silent. It was the beginning of a cocoon of silence that I wove around me in order to make good on my promise to Mama. Sadness took over—the same sadness that glazed over the eyes of my siblings. I decided that silence was the only way forward. I sacrificed my siblings to pave the way for my own escape—biding my time until Mama could rescue me. The others would have to find their own modes of escape.

The years passed at a plodding pace. I continued to sleep gripping that knife under my pillow—ignoring the guilt gnawing at every aspect of my being about how I didn't use that knife to protect my sister. Ed Madden was very good at cornering her when no one else was around, making sure that no one ever witnessed these assaults. Even though Zonnetta refused to listen to me, I think Ed Madden knew that if she ever caught him in the act, it would be over for him. Denial is much easier when you don't have to contradict your own eyes. Zonnetta had already gone through a couple of husbands. It was pretty obvious that Ed Madden wouldn't last forever. I guess he figured that he would take what he could while he was there.

Mama once gave me a tiny pink radio. I added it to my prized possessions, propping it up next to my globe. When I was a teenager, a new sound began taking over the airwaves. The contagious rhythm of the Motor City gripped the nation, helping to dissolve the monopoly that white performers had over pop music. Dancing to Motown in my bedroom—the sound muffled to not disturb Zonnetta and Ed Madden—was the only thing that could calm my soul enough to sleep each night. It was also the one thing that I could share with my sisters. Dancing meant freedom. It was my spiritual practice. It kept me grounded in a world that seemingly wanted to tear apart every fiber of my being. My childhood would've been void of all joy if I didn't have a space to dance, or my globe and library books to buttress my daydreaming. In fact, to this day I still dance to Motown when 88.3 plays the greatest hits on Saturdays.

Surviving off these gifts, I somehow finished high school. On graduation day, however, I did not think about all the knowledge that I had learned and how it would prepare me for the world. I just wondered if Mama was really going to save me like she had promised all those years ago. She had come into town for graduation. Zonnetta hadn't even bothered to show up to the ceremony, which was probably for the best. Mama greeted me after I made my way across the stage and whispered for me to head home and pack my most important possessions. She was inviting me to stay with her for a couple of days and would meet me at the bus station that evening.

I thought it odd that I would need my most important possessions for a short visit. I really hoped that it meant what I prayed it did—that I was finally leaving Kansas for good. But after suffering so much disappointment in my life, I didn't want to place too much faith in this moment. I also didn't want Zonnetta to suspect anything. I needed it to appear that I really was going to Missouri for just a couple of days.

When I went home that afternoon, I found Robert sitting at the kitchen table. I didn't know what to say to him, so I headed to my room and found the overnight bag that I usually took to Mama's house. I rolled up a few outfits and underwear into a tiny ball and stuffed them in. I frowned when I saw that there was no room left for my globe and pink radio. I realized that neither Zonnetta nor Ed Madden was home and opted to take a small suitcase that was buried in the bottom of the hall closet that could fit everything I needed. I then prayed that they wouldn't walk through the door before I left, as I smuggled out the few things that had kept me alive all these years.

As I headed toward the kitchen, I hid my suitcase behind the couch before telling Robert to let Zonnetta know that I was going to Mama's for a couple of days. As I mentioned before, just because Robert had trouble in school didn't mean that he was stupid. He searched my eyes with a knowing look and told me to take care of myself. I didn't want our last moment together to be so devoid of emotion, so I grabbed his shoulders and pulled him to me. I didn't know if I would ever see him again. Then without a word, I went back to the couch, retrieved my bag, and walked out the front door for the last time. I met Mama at the bus station and we boarded our bus to Missouri. As I crossed the state line, I vowed never to set foot in Kansas again. I almost kept my word.

Chapter 2: California Living

"Whisky A Go-Go, Los Angeles," 1964 © Julian Wasser. Courtesy of Craig Krull Gallery, Santa Monica, California. Used with permission.

Alvenia has nothing lying around in her apartment that conjures the mood of the sixties, but her vivid depictions of the Whisky a Go Go allow me to imagine myself walking in Alvenia's high heels, as she navigated a new town with a new lease on life. The Whisky was the first scene that Alvenia ever described for me during her storytelling sessions, making it very clear what a pivotal moment entering the club had represented in her life. Mere days after I became her roommate in 2014, she recounted her rebirth in Los Angeles. The Whisky was where she could finally do what she loved *most—dancing and she could do so without having to hide her joy from the disapproving eyes of her mother or from an unrelenting city that dictated in which spaces she could and couldn't exist. While no memento of her life in the sixties remains in Alvenia's possession, when I found this 1964 photo of opening night at the Whisky—where a racially-mixed group of people line up for what will turn out to be the beginning of over half a century of music and merriment—Alvenia's place in history became that much more tangible in my mind.*

Mama Beatrice had never intended for me to stay with her in Missouri for very long. She must've known that she wouldn't be able to protect me if I remained in such proximity to the family that I sought to write out of my life. And the people in Missouri had the same mentality as those in Kansas. Nothing was going to change in my life unless I could physically separate myself from these places. In many ways, my story started off similarly to the six million other African Americans undertaking the Great Migration between 1910-1970.[1] I didn't know that that was what I was doing when I left Kansas in 1962, but neither did they.

Mama had been in touch with an aunt who I had never heard of and secured my passage to Los Angeles before I even stepped foot in Missouri. Within days of escaping Kansas, I was on a plane for the first time, but it felt like I had been on one my whole life. I felt so comfortable in the air, so at ease – I can't explain it other than that I was born to fly. It was after I landed that some apprehension crept in. The plane had been

---

1. Also known as the Great Northward Migration, African Americans moved from the US South to the Northeast, Midwest, and West to escape racial discrimination, segregation, and terror as well as to improve their economic opportunities.

my refuge. It was what spirited me away from my childhood hell, but what if I was exchanging one hell for another? The people I was about to meet were supposedly family too and I had not had good luck with family.

Uncle Chuck, Aunt Virginia, and Cousin Larry all met me at LAX. Virginia had flaming red hair and a personality to match. She was exuberant, and love overflowed from her, like lava from her molten core. Uncle Chuck had a huge laugh that bellowed after he told jokes. Cousin Larry was less boisterous, perhaps even a bit shy, but he was poised and could disarm anyone with his smile. Looking out the car window as we left the airport, I was in awe of the massive highways that coiled around Los Angeles like the tentacles of a giant squid. Uncle Chuck talked about how he loved to cook and loved to eat and was going to love preparing all his favorite meals for me, because it was obvious to him that I hadn't eaten much in years. Aunt Virginia kept interrupting, "Chuck, let me talk. You're overwhelming the poor girl!" I just sat there basking in the love that exuded from this family. It was a love that expected nothing in return.

When we arrived at their home in Pacoima, I instantly admired the palm trees, the birds of paradise, and the avocados. But most of all, I was in awe of the sky. I didn't remember seeing the sky when I was growing up. It must have been there, but perhaps I never bothered to look up. I always trained my eyes on the pavement in front of me because accidentally catching the wrong person's gaze could have deadly repercussions. Nothing good ever happened when you looked up. As I stared at the sky, I felt like I was being born to it. I was being made anew and that was a wonderful feeling.

Uncle Chuck had separated from Larry's mother when Larry was a baby. Larry remained in Arkansas with his mother and Uncle Chuck eventually married Aunt Virginia—Zonnetta's sister—and lived in Chicago until 1959 when they decided to go out west. Larry joined his father and stepmother during his senior year of high school when medical issues caused him to seek out doctors in Los Angeles. He wound up staying with Chuck and Virginia for the rest of high school, graduated, and then started at Los Angeles Valley College in 1961.

When they interacted, however, you would never have known that Virginia was Larry's stepmother. She treated him like her own child. From the beginning, she offered me that same generosity, never making me feel that I did not belong and never making me question whether I was deserving of her love. She just loved. And so did Chuck. And so did Larry. I had a true mother and father for the first time and I gained another brother who would end up being not only my closest family member, but also my best friend for the rest of my life. I had never had a friend before. Being able to confide in someone, when I could only rely on myself before, allowed me to experience the simple pleasure of not having the weight of the world bearing down on me all the time. I settled in my room that night and felt like I had been given a second chance at life. My time in Los Angeles helped me create a different understanding of family and friendship.

Mama's globe sat on the nightstand next to my twin-size bed. This was the first time that I had my own room. It was so much fun to spin that globe as fast as it could go, then drag my finger over its textured surface like the diamond-tipped needle of a 45. Wherever it stopped, I would say, that's where I'm going someday. To be able to voice these dreams out loud, without anyone overhearing me and scornfully laughing, was one of the nicest things about living in Los Angeles.

Across from the globe was my only other prized possession, the pink radio. It was slightly scuffed from overuse. When I turned that thing on, I would spin like that globe, dancing my way to another planet and forgetting about the hate and turmoil of the reality I had just escaped. While I was a dancing fiend, I was never able to learn the latest dances in Kansas because I had neither the time, money, nor freedom to go out. But in Los Angeles, I managed to go out every night to satiate my need to dance.

One night in early 1964, I stumbled upon a new hit in town, the Whisky A Go Go on Sunset Boulevard. Sunset Boulevard! Hah! Comparing the glitz of that street to the dusty dreariness of Cleveland Avenue always elicited a chuckle from me. The Whisky made me shout with glee. It was my drug. I went there religiously throughout the sixties. There, I could dance like a wild woman. I didn't even need a partner. Actually, I preferred the freedom and creativity of dancing to my own groove. This club was the spot where go-go dancing supposedly originated—a style of dancing where you weren't expected to dance with anyone if you didn't want to. Joanie Labine, the first deejay at the Whisky, would get everyone in the mood for go-go dancing as she strutted her stuff while spinning the records. There's no wonder that the Whisky became the heart of my new home in Los Angeles.

On one occasion, there were two beautiful people, James Finney and Betty Mabry, dancing front and center. Finney had plaits that tickled his waist as they vibrated in time with the music. His braids moved to the beat while he danced between it. I had never seen plaits like these before or such long hair on a man. Betty, not to be outdone, had this stunning, gigantic Afro that bounced in sync with every jolt of her body. After watching them from the corner of the dance floor, I decided to go over to them. Although I risked sounding like a country mouse, I couldn't help but gush, "Excuse me. You are the most beautiful Black people I've ever seen. I hope you don't mind my saying that."

Finney smiled magnanimously and replied, "You don't belong here in California. You should come to New York. We live in New York." He then gave me his phone number before we each returned to dancing in our own worlds.

I didn't know at that moment how influential Finney would be in my life, both because of his dexterity as a hair stylist and his ability to orchestrate human connections through his gregarious nature. We eventually cultivated a friendship that would blossom and thrive until his passing. Meanwhile, I saw Betty a few times throughout the years. She went on to marry Miles Davis, influencing his style and music before their rocky divorce.[2] She was an amazing singer, but sadly became a recluse until her passing in 2022. Regardless, Betty and Finney transformed my image of what it meant to be Black in America. The Blackness I was used to was one of struggle and survival. One of diverted glances and moving out the way. One of resignation and timidity. But their Blackness thrived. They were unapologetically Black even when surrounded by whiteness. Their brightness dwarfed everything around them. Such style. Such

---

2. See Crowhurst, "Forgotten Women."

poise. Such power. Meeting them was the beginning of my personal awakening.

The Whisky also brought me face to face with international Blackness through the stylish bands from the far reaches of the globe that performed there. Black Africans could interact with Black Americans, bridging, through music, the divide that geography and divergent histories had wrought. Betty would often hang out with Hugh Masekela and even though I wasn't as polished and put together as women like Betty, I sometimes got to mingle with musical geniuses as well. Hugh, the father of South African jazz and author of anti-apartheid protest songs, was one of the acts that had a lasting impression on me. Still raw from my experience with American segregation and racial hatred from my childhood in Kansas, I was horrified by the oppression suffered by Blacks in South Africa. When he wasn't performing, we would talk about all sorts of things and during his stint in California, we became friends.

Hugh and I had originally met outside of my interactions with Betty, when he came up to me between his sets one night he was performing at the Whisky. I was dancing like crazy, completely oblivious to my surroundings and he wanted to know who the spindly woman that was creating her own gravitational pull in the middle of the dance floor was. He asked if I wanted to hang with him, his manager Stewart Levine, and some of their friends on the beach after his gig was over. I had never been to the beach because living in the valley didn't afford me much of an opportunity. My daily routine consisted of going from home to Los Angeles Valley College, where I was a student with Larry, to work—I had picked up some babysitting hours—to the Whisky. Before I moved to California, I just assumed that everybody in the whole state lived on the beach. When I settled into Los Angeles, I realized how wrong I was.

California is a sprawling state that includes vast swaths of inland towns and farms, but even for people living in a coastal city like Los Angeles, accessing the water can be a luxury. Los Angeles is just so large and so socially segregated that kids born a mere ten miles from the coast might never feel what it's like to walk on sand in their lifetime, especially in the sixties.

I took Hugh and Stewart up on their offer and set out with them in their fancy ride once the Whisky had shut down for the night. I could tell that it was the nicest car that I had ever been in, because it was the first time that my long legs fit comfortably somewhere. We, along with many of their friends, drove to the hills overlooking Malibu Beach and set out a picnic blanket—sharing stories about our lives and journeys amidst the sound of waves crashing against the shoreline. Hugh had met Stewart in 1961 when they were at the Manhattan School of Music. They had formed their own record label, Chisa—the Zulu word for "burn"—and were excited to tell me all about their musical plans. I was following the conversation intently until someone in the entourage started passing a joint around. Thus, Hugh has the dubious distinction of being the first and only person with whom I tried drugs. I'm actually grateful for the experience, because I think it protected me from the debauchery and overindulgence that would claim the lives of so many people who I met in my years in the fashion and music industries.[3]

Apparently, my mind is not made for any sort of mind-altering substances. As the joint reached my nervous fingers, I strategized how to be cool. Here I was, surrounded by an international crowd of some of the

---

3. For more information about Hugh Masekela and Stewart Levine, see their interview through *Design Indaba*.

"baddest" people the planet could produce. After spending a lifetime in solitude and isolation, I was ready to connect with people on any level I could. I was a good study and had been intently observing how everyone casually raised the joint to their lips, barely parting them, just enough to take a drag. They would then hold their breath for a few seconds before exhaling smoke through their noses. It looked simple enough; however, I was not prepared for the coughing attack that overtook me, which divulged my newbie status. I had obviously missed some steps during my observation.

The group laughed, but not in a way that made me feel dumb. One of the women in the group then showed me her technique. When the joint circled around the next time, I was ready. I managed to keep my throat from convulsing this time but was a little underwhelmed by the sensation. I wasn't experiencing the mellowing effect that everyone raved about. Nothing was changing inside me. A few minutes passed before suddenly I had this overwhelming urge to be unrestrained. I stood up from the blanket where we were sitting and started to take off my pink blouse.

Hugh said with an amused tone, "Alvenia! What are you doing?"

I remember laughing back, "I don't know, Hugh, I just need to be free. I'm freeing myself."

They took the joint from me and threw another blanket my way. Hugh then wrapped it around me and said, "First time?"

I just chuckled. When I was in control of my senses again, I was astounded by the ability for a tiny bundle of grass to make me lose so much control. I learned my stuff quickly though. I was obsessed with not doing the wrong thing, especially against myself and I knew at that moment that drugs would not be a part of my life. No matter what substances were floating around in all my years in fashion and music, I would flash on the embarrassment that I felt that night. I have not touched a joint since and passed up any other drugs that came my way.

⌇⌇⌇ ❀ ⌇⌇⌇

Thinking about all those nights at the Whisky with people like Hugh, Betty, Finney, and countless others, I came to see the club as my opening to a Black cosmopolitan world I didn't know existed. At the same time, it also challenged my understanding of Black-white relations. I could interact with white people in a way that I never could in Kansas. It was a strange but liberating feeling. For instance, I met John Von Neumann at the Whisky and he's the reason why I am the person I am today. While Finney and Betty showed me the type of person I could be, John opened the world to me, a world that sculpted the person who I would become.

One night, I was dancing, lost in my own frenzy. Suddenly, Mario Maglieri, the manager and eventual owner of the Whisky, tapped me on the shoulder. That was the signal to go out the back door. I was underage and if the police ever arrived, I needed a quick escape. I moved to grab my jacket and sneak out, but he stopped me. "I have someone I'd like you to meet." He smiled. Adrenaline still pumping from having been ready to run, I followed him to the VIP section where Mr. Von Neumann was sitting with actor George Hamilton and an actress who I did not recognize. Mr. Von Neumann requested that I sit down. I hesitated, because I was out of my element in this section of the club that was reserved for the city's elite, but Mario assured me that he was harmless.

"You're a wonderful dancer," Mr. Von Neumann stated with a sincerity in his voice that took me slightly aback. However, I didn't appreciate being abruptly plucked from my dancing so that some fancy man in the VIP section could pay me a compliment.

I unceremoniously replied, "You brought me over here for this?" I then pushed the chair back, swiftly turned on my heels, and returned to my kingdom. I didn't even think about it. There was nothing that I wanted to do more than dance, dance, dance, until it was time for me to retreat to the Valley.

Besides, when I was dancing, all was right with the world. A sense of calm would wash over my whole body—a stark contrast to the frenetic energy of the music. All worries and fears vacated my mind, leaving me contentedly oblivious to the world outside. My heart would then beat in time to the funkiness of the rhythm, grounding me even as I felt like I was levitating above the dance floor. Each time I danced I recreated the feeling that I had all those years ago when the little voice in my head had convinced me that everything would be okay. This comforting presence would remain with me for the rest of my life, making itself known whenever I needed guidance.

Around closing time, I waved to Mario, grabbed my jacket for real this time, walked out to the parking lot at Clark and Sunset, and hopped on my little motorcycle, which I called Putt Putt because of the noise it made when struggling uphill. As Putt Putt tackled the hill, I passed Mr. Von Neumann in his car. I started chiding myself for being so rude earlier. Dancing had that effect on me, as I didn't allow anything to stand in the way of me and the music. I slowed to approach. As he rolled down his window, I apologized for my rudeness. But he stopped me by repeating his earlier words, "You're a wonderful dancer." But this time he added, "Will you teach me how to dance?"

Will you teach me how to dance? "Everyone knows how to dance," was all I could think of as a reply.

"Please. Will you teach me how to dance? I'll pay you." He gave me his card that read Volkswagen, Culver City. "My secretary's name is Mary. Think about it. I'm very serious. I would like to learn how to dance."

I took the card but said nothing. He finally drove away.

I really wanted to act cool, but I kept catching myself thinking about this opportunity, about how teaching dance could be a good way to earn extra money. I was doing all these odd jobs to help pay for my studies and chip in around the house. While my hesitation stemmed from not believing that people had to be taught how to dance—something that came naturally to me—in my naïveté, it didn't cross my mind how strange a proposition like this could seem to someone else. A rich, established man asking a slightly underage woman to be his dance instructor seemed like a genuine request to me.

After a few days, I gathered the courage to call Mary. Nervous, I began to blabber about how I had met Mr. Von Neumann at the Whisky, but she cut me off, "John mentioned that someone might call about teaching him how to dance. You must be the young lady he met."

I was stunned that she was expecting my call and didn't know how to proceed.

"John would like to invite you to dinner." Her words shook me from my momentary daze. I had never been invited to dinner at someone's house before.

"Well, I go to school, so it has to fit with my schedule."

"That can be arranged," she replied, then gave me directions on how to get to his house in Beverly Hills.

A few days later, I ventured into this uncharted territory, feeling out of place amidst the backdrop of sheer opulence. I was wearing the simple black slacks I usually wore to the Whisky along with a hand-me-down shirt crowded with blocks of colorful geometric patterns that my Aunt Virginia had given me to help jumpstart my wardrobe. As she liked to put it, we weren't in Kansas no more. I needed a new look to match my new life.

Given that my aunt and uncle lived in Pacoima, before that evening I had never been further than the Whisky on Sunset. Beverly Hills began after that point. It's like crossing a border. Mulholland Drive deposits you at long driveways that grant you passage into giant homes protected by vibrant plant life. I parked Putt Putt and started walking up a brick path. As I approached the front door, I could see all of Los Angeles to my left. The sun had almost completely set, leaving a halo emanating from the tall buildings of the city center. There must have been thousands of lights. Living in the city that had something for everyone, I had gone from Kansas to the top. I pushed the doorbell and this wonderful, tall Black man—a butler with white gloves named Buddy Anderson—opened the door and let me in.

As I entered, I was slightly paralyzed by the grandeur of the home. The windows stretched from floor to ceiling, showing off the same magnificent vista of mountains and high-rise buildings that you could see from the brick path. Buddy, also called Buddha, spoke to me and suddenly I realized that my mouth had been agape, betraying the awe that had washed over me. "Would you like to take a seat? John will arrive in a second."

"Thank you." I felt the need to curtsy but somehow restrained myself.

Mr. Von Neumann made his entrance and asked what I would like to drink. I was not very sophisticated in this regard, or in my food knowledge for that matter, so I responded with, "I'll have whatever you're having." This little phrase became my motto. I said it every time he asked what I would like, because I never had any clue what was laid out before me. So that's how I had my first glass of champagne.

While we waited for dinner, Mr. Von Neumann showed me his music studio, a large room with an impressive number of turntables and speakers. More notably, it had marvelous acoustics. The whole house was wired for entertaining the big parties he threw. He loved music, and it was mind-boggling how much he knew about it. He then explained that while he knew a lot about music, he knew nothing about dancing. He was excited that I was willing to try to teach him.

As we circled back to the dining room, he announced that it was time to eat. Buddha pulled out a chair for me at one end of this long table, adorned with an intricate lace tablecloth. As I was getting comfortable, I saw him pull out the chair for Mr. Von Neumann at the other end of the table. He was so far away! Buddha asked if I would like lamb. I had never had lamb. I was a little perplexed by the food options and the distance so I asked, "Mr. Von Neumann, may I come closer?"

He chuckled, "Yes you may. And please call me John." So, I got up and plopped next to him as gracefully as this Kansas girl could. He started naming different types of fish and after each offering, I replied with my tag line, "I'll have what you're having." This tickled John to no end. He would tease me for years after that once we reconnected in a land far, far away. He also had an amused look when he realized that I knew nothing about silverware. Why would anyone need more than one knife, fork and spoon? He tried to explain the differences and their particular uses, but that was one thing that I never caught on. I couldn't really bring myself to care which fork was used for salads.

Even if I was somewhat of an unwilling pupil when it came to dining etiquette, it was a wonderful dinner. I had never experienced anything like it. Halfway through, John asked me what I wanted more than anything in the world. Thinking about how my grandmother had asked me the same question all those years ago, I told him that I simply wanted the world. John was an amazing listener, nodding compassionately as I mentioned my globe and how as a child, I would clutch it close to my heart, cradling the treasure that it was. I laid out my dreams of traveling; I wanted to see what other people were like, what they ate, how they dressed, what made them get up every morning. I hated my life growing up and so I learned to invent these fantasies to get through each day. From an early age, I was never looking for anything in particular, just trying to find my way. But I was convinced that I could discover these answers by experiencing how others understood the world. I had already learned so much just by escaping Kansas. The world must be able to teach me even more. Little did I know at that time that he was cataloguing these dreams and putting a plan into place to make them come alive. He would one day give me the world.

In our first class, a few days later, I found out that he only knew one step—side to side. Actually, it wasn't even side to side. He would just sort of list to the right. I was glad that he was soon leaving on a three-month business trip to Europe because it allowed me time to formulate a game plan. Transforming this man into someone who could keep up on the dance floor would be a monumental task. Upon his return, Mary helped me set up a routine so that I could fit in dance lessons without them interfering with my studying and in a way that wouldn't raise suspicions from Chuck and Virginia as to what I was up to. As understanding as they were, I figured they would find it strange that I was spending so much time with someone so far from my social circle.

Looking back on it all these years later, perhaps I had sensed how our platonic relationship could be misread by others. I seldom interacted with the people I met at the Whisky outside. I seldom interacted with people inside the Whisky either, for that matter, since I was there for the music. I was not consciously aware of how our friendship might be seen as a social transgression in some ways. In the end, I'm glad that I was clueless to the optics of such a friendship. After closing myself off to the world and having so much of the world closed off to me, I was confronted with a man who genuinely enjoyed my presence and valued my skills. He was someone who treated me with respect and never once hinted at something sexual. I now know that our friendship would not have worked if there had been an ulterior motive. All I knew about sexual entanglements were those linked to forced vulgarities. It would take years before I could even imagine myself as a sexual being, regardless of how people saw me. To meet someone like John, who could give me the space to heal as a person, was truly a sign that the world had decided to give me a break.

Several months passed, and I could see gradual improvement in John's dancing. He had taken to calling me Venus—a marked improvement over Orangutan. I also noticed the strange little smile he had on his face all the time. I don't believe it meant anything in particular; I think he was just happy with life. He had so much money but wasn't attached to it. He just wanted to enjoy life and that meant sharing his wealth in ways that would benefit others. I thought it was a great model for how I would behave if I ever had money. I was amazed at how shy and humble he was and couldn't imagine how someone could live in a house like that and not be a massive snob. As we spent time together, I began to piece together the incredible life he had made for himself.

America had been good to him. He had fled Europe in 1938 during the Nazi Anschluss, when he saw Germany annex his native Austria. Landing in New York City, he stayed there for a of couple years before the bombing of Pearl Harbor convinced him to sign up for the US Army. His fluency in German made him a valuable asset to US Intelligence and while he was performing his military duties behind enemy lines, he learned much about German transportation engineering.

After the war, he moved to California where he eventually founded Competition Motors Distributors and began racing in the California Sports Car Club to advertise his merchandise. Using his knowledge from his army days, he added German Porsche and Volkswagen to the lineup. He also became a top racer for Ferrari on the California scene and is credited with being the father of the Ferrari roadster, the Golden State. At the time, anyone who knew anything about competitive car racing or fancy cars would know the name John Von Neumann.[4]

After a couple of decades in the US, however, Europe was calling him, so he finally returned, settling down outside of Geneva, Switzerland. When John went back to Europe for good in the mid-sixties, I missed him deeply, because I had never said goodbye to someone who respected me so much. I had already mourned the fact that I probably wouldn't see Mama again. Yet, she felt like a part of me, so I never really saw her as gone. But John seemed like a blip on the screen, some sort of waking

---

4. See Pietrowicz, "John Von Neumann," for more information.

dream that I wasn't really sure had happened. This translated into an immense loss. I worried that I would never see him again, especially once I decided to try my luck in New York City.

After a few more years on the West Coast, I began to realize that Los Angeles no longer wowed or awed me. The Whisky was still jamming, but the California music scene that was such a juggernaut in the early to mid-sixties was losing out to the allure of New York City. I had shed the stigma of being the backwards girl from Kansas who felt out of her league in a big city. I had stumbled on some confidence, partially by surrounding myself with people who respected me and told me that I could go far and I began to dare to dream larger and wider.

Chapter 3: Encountering Europe

Fig. 4. Alvenia lounging. Original by Leonardo De Vega. By Maya Angela Smith.

Fig. 5 Alvenia in Europe. Original by Gerald Parkes. By Maya Angela Smith.

When I came across these photos of Alvenia in 2014, I found myself wondering why she never became a supermodel. These images display the same grace, poise, and ethereal beauty as the biggest names in the business. When I asked Alvenia to tell me a little about these photos—convinced they were from her modeling days in Europe—I was shocked to find out that they were taken in the eighties, years after her modeling career was over. They had such a timeless quality.

Alvenia's friend, Leonardo De Vega, took the first photo (Fig. 4) one night when Alvenia was feeling depressed. A photographer and make-up artist, he told her to pick out her favorite dress and to come over for a glass of champagne and a photo shoot. Since Leonardo only lived half a block away, she decided to wear her bedroom slippers lined with tufts of marabou feathers for the walk over. They matched the satin nightgown that she chose for her outfit. It was through Leonardo that Alvenia learned that all you needed for a truly impressive look was to focus on the eyes and lips. To this day, she only wears lipstick and a little color to accentuate her eyes. When Alvenia saw the photos that Leonardo took of her that evening for the first time, she teared up, because she had convinced herself that she would look terrible. He proved to her how beautiful she was no matter the occasion or her mood.

The second photo (Fig. 5) was taken on a trip to the south of France, years after Alvenia had first stepped on European soil. She was walking to a restaurant with Gerald, a person that would play a major role in Alvenia's story and as they passed by the intricately carved wooden doors of a church, he captured Alvenia doing what she does best, looking fierce.

In early 1969, I went to New York on my own, with a little money saved up from all my odd jobs and with the blessing of Chuck, Virginia, and Larry. James Finney had told me that if I ever made it to New York, there was this happening place called the Scene on 46th Street and 8th Avenue. The day I landed, after dropping my paltry belongings on the bed I was renting at a tiny hostel, I made my first entrance at the Scene. Nestled in the heart of the Theatre district, the Scene originally attracted actors, musicians, and other theatre types looking for a place to unwind each night after performing on Broadway. It eventually began enjoying the patronage of the who's who of New York once it became known as *the* place for late night jam sessions with some of the biggest names in showbusiness. Jimi Hendrix, Pink Floyd, the Doors, Richard Pryor, Liza

Minelli, and many others graced the stage in both impromptu sessions and planned performances.[1]

Nobodies like me couldn't just walk up and enter. You had to get past the boldly dressed and imposing Teddy—the bouncer whose last name I never learned—before being met at the door by Steve Paul, the owner himself. Steve would usually tell some joke at your expense and if you responded in a way that he deemed acceptable, he might let you in. If I had gone there directly from Kansas, there's no way he would've let me pass. But I learned to cloak myself in an understated yet perceptible swagger when I needed to play the part and since I had long legs and a short skirt—this was the late sixties right before mini-skirts went out of fashion—I didn't have to wait too long to be let in.

The place wasn't what I imagined a New York club to be. Steve had taken a five-bedroom townhouse marked by a maze of adjoining rooms and transformed it into a chic yet cozy setting. Stumbling through the twists and turns of the floorplan had a dizzying effect, especially with the smoke from cigarettes and joints clouding the air. My quest to find Finney was a lot like an Easter egg hunt. You had to explore every nook and cranny to see who was lounging about in darkened corners. However, I should've known that Finney would be out on the dance floor and I finally found him in the room farthest from the front door.

"You made it!" Finney exclaimed when I caught his eye, acting as if we had it scheduled to meet on this specific day. He didn't seem surprised that I'd shown up in New York City out of the blue, a year or so after we first met. Somehow, he always knew that I would make my way to

---

1. For details about the Scene, see "Making the (Steve Paul) Scene" and Martin's "Steve Paul Dies."

this city that would become home. Meanwhile, I was amazed that on a random night, I found him just like he said I would. I didn't even need to use his phone number that I had saved all that time. After we caught up over a drink, he chided lovingly, "I told you Los Angeles was too small. It was only a matter of time before you came to your senses." He then asked me what I needed to set up my life in New York. I told him I wanted to go to school and how I needed a job to pay for it. He said that he would put his feelers out.

With Finney's help, I got a job as a waitress at a pizzeria on the Upper West Side. Johnny McLaughlin, a guitarist from South Yorkshire, England, was a regular there. He had just moved to the United States to join the band Lifetime, headed by Tony Williams, an American Jazz drummer best known for his work with Miles Davis. One day, Johnny and I got to talking and when he mentioned he was in search of a roommate, I told him that I was dying to find a more stable living environment. On the spot, Johnny extended the offer to move into his apartment on 76th near Columbus Circle.

In this little apartment complex, Tony Williams lived next door to us, as well as Dave Holland, whose claim to fame was being Miles Davis's bassist. I wouldn't meet Miles until years later, but I knew him vicariously through the company I kept. I was particularly happy to meet my new neighbors Pat Hartley and Dick Fontaine, who lived across from me. Pat was a gorgeous Black actress, barely out of her teens, who had worked with Andy Warhol on several occasions. Dick was her long-haired, white, British, movie director husband who dedicated much of his career to documenting African American music. They split their time between New York and London when they weren't travelling to far-flung destinations, so I was fortunate enough to get to know them during the short time that we overlapped.

I settled into a routine. During the day, I worked at a couple of restaurants to save up money to enroll at the Fashion Institute of Technology. At night, I went dancing at the Scene and crossed paths with musical legends. I was quite content with my life, although I would occasionally miss John and our dancing classes. I sometimes wondered what he was up to and whether we would ever meet again.

One afternoon, in spring of 1969, Johnny came to my room to inform me of a telegram that had arrived for me at the Western Union on 72nd and Broadway. I was taken aback when the telegram read "Alvenia Bridges, leaving on a one-way flight to Geneva on Swiss Air." It then contained instructions on how to pick up my ticket. I would find out later that John had hired a private investigator to track me down. In this moment, I was so over the moon that I just dropped everything—not even considering how rash my decision was and the possible consequences of such a move.

At that moment, I just thought about how I would pull off such a quick, international move. Pat had to talk me through how to get a passport. I went about preparing for this surprise opportunity while being in a super haze from the spontaneity of it all. I didn't have much to pack because I considered myself a nomad. Since I was in this phase where I regularly wore suede cowboy chaps and feathers in my hair, I threw multiple versions of this odd sartorial practice into my suitcase along with a couple of party dresses. My passport arrived right before my scheduled departure. While I hadn't been in New York for more than a couple of months, I was still sad to leave my community, which had welcomed me so openly in New York. Pat hugged me and told me to reach out to her if I was ever in London and needed a place to stay. I thanked her and headed on my way.

In what seemed like no time at all from the moment I received that telegram, I was on a flight to Switzerland. I had only been on domestic flights before. Flying meant freedom: the freedom to explore, the freedom to choose, the freedom to grow. Flying was so wrapped up in my dream of liberation, where traveling the world encapsulated the possibility for escape and renewal, that I didn't mind hovering several thousand miles over the Atlantic for hours on end.

The flight was also the first moment I had to actually think about what I was doing and question whether uprooting to Europe made any sense. My dream, ever since Mama Beatrice gave me that globe, was to see the world. But what was I really doing? I started to second guess myself, but then, out of nowhere, the voice in my head resurfaced. This time it said nothing more than a resounding "Go!" At that moment, I knew I was going to have to learn to trust the Spirit in order to survive in the world. That I needed to take chances if I wanted to transform my wild dreams into reality.

What would it be like to see John again? He would become the first man that I ever allowed myself to feel anything for. The first twenty-five years of my life I had numbed myself, not entertaining the fact that there could be healthy relationships between men and women. That is what happens when you teach yourself to grow up without a mother and without guidance, other than learning from other people's mistakes and from the gentle nudging of a mysterious voice in your head. Every man that Zonnetta brought into our lives was a mistake. She was the last person I wanted to emulate.

I arrived in Geneva and got off the plane in my feathers and chaps. John was waiting for me, holding a sign, face plastered with a sweet smirk. He took my hand, which had an electrifying effect that I hadn't expected and which helped to invigorate me after a sleepless journey. As my senses slowly became attuned to my surroundings, I distinctly remember everyone looking at me. I wanted to believe it was for my unconventional clothing style, but deep down I knew it was because I was the only person of color in this little airport. However, it didn't matter how annoyed I was with the constant stares or how tired I was from transatlantic sleep deprivation, I perked up completely when we got to John's canary yellow Rolls Royce. I had never seen a Rolls Royce before and its chrome finish almost eclipsed the sun. His driver opened my door and I slipped in.

From the airport, we drove around Lake Geneva. We would be staying on the Lausanne side, but he took us around the French side so that he could show me the lake from a different perspective. We eventually arrived at the village of Versoix, where he lived right on the lake. When we pulled into the driveway, four or five people approached the car. Buddha, who had remained a part of John's household all these years, opened my side door. It was the most beautiful surprise. After giving me a huge hug, Buddha took me inside and introduced me to John's wife, the first of several that I would meet over the years as he flitted in and out of my life. John then explained the concept of jetlag to me, before showing me my room so that I could rest and get ready for the evening festivities he had planned. Jetlag or not, there was no way I could rest, so I sat at the edge of my bed looking out on Lake Geneva's majestic waterscape.

It was the beginning of summer, so the evenings had plenty of daylight. We met several of John's friends at this club-like restaurant on the lake. They all spoke French and while I couldn't understand what they were saying, I picked up that John was telling them about my dancing. I wanted to contribute to the conversation, but the language barrier and the jetlag, which had finally caught up to me, were too daunting and I slowly drifted into my own world.

When we returned from dinner, John informed me that I would be in Geneva for a week before his driver would take me to Portofino, Italy, for a job opportunity. He gave me a bicycle that I could use to explore the town on my own throughout the week, but first thing on the agenda was to fix my wardrobe. Good to his word, he took me shopping the following morning and made sure I never stepped out of the house another day wearing cowboy chaps and feathers. I learned then that the smirk he greeted me with at the airport was hiding the plan he was formulating in his mind when he saw me step off the plane. In all the time I knew John, I never saw him angry at anyone. He was always smiling. If you did something wrong, he smiled. But if you needed it, you got fixed. I never saw my chaps again.

The following week, John's driver and I embarked on our Italian trip. I was very uncomfortable sitting in the back of the car—not from lack of space but because I saw no reason why we had to be segregated in such a way. I convinced the driver to let me sit in the front seat with him. While Portofino was only about 250 miles away, we took the scenic route over a couple of days, stopping in little villages all throughout northern Italy. My favorite part was eating in the mom-and-pop restaurants and familiarizing myself with the local cuisine. I fell in love with gnocchi, which I never learned to pronounce correctly. My tongue just refused to produce that "nya" sound at the beginning of words. No one ever corrected me when I said "occhi" instead. They just laughed and chalked it up to my being an American. While I might not have been able to pronounce everything I ate, it didn't keep me from enjoying each dish. Italy truly has the best food in the world.

When we approached Portofino, on the Italian Riviera, I was stunned by its beauty. The village opened onto the harbor. We took a little road that I would soon take every day on my bright orange moped, a fine machine but no substitute for my beloved Putt Putt. As you ascend the hill into town, there's a little church at the top. The driver dropped me off at a three-story building, in which there was a tiny studio apartment that I would call home for the summer. I loved to people-watch and became excited when I opened my window and saw how it framed the expanse of the harbor.

A couple of hours after settling in, I heard a rap on the door. The Swiss restaurateur Peppo Vanini, who would make his mark on New York City a decade later with club Xenon, had arrived to take me to his current disco, Il Covo di Nord-Est, a few miles away. As we drove up the coastline toward Santa Margherita Liguria, I couldn't get over how crystal clear the water was with its swirling hues of cobalt and cerulean blue. The club was unlike any place I'd ever seen. It was a cave carved out of the natural rockface, open to the water. John had convinced Peppo to give me a job as a deejay and that's how I started working in Italy. I had spun a couple times before but had no formal training. But people would come all over to listen to me spin and watch me dance behind the turn tables.

The club attracted people from cities such as Genoa, especially now that it was summer. Everyone wanted to hang out on the Mediterranean.

Il Covo was immensely popular. People with lots of money could park their yachts in the harbor and swim up to the disco. The entrance fee in 1969 was exorbitant at 100,000 lira, around $60, which ensured that the clientele met Vanini's high expectations. Performers such as Frank Sinatra, Sammy Davis Jr., Barry White, and Grace Jones all passed through at some point. If you were on the Mediterranean, it was the place to be. I got to do what I loved best, listen to music, dance, and learn about people and their fascinating lives.[2]

One afternoon while eating lunch at Il Covo, which attracted a more laid-back crowd during the day, I began to talk to a young German woman and her brother who were visiting from Dusseldorf. She had waist-length platinum hair that appeared completely natural and she and her brother were as sweet as honey. I enjoyed hearing about their lives. Monika Dannemann had been a figure skater, competing at the German Figure Skating Championships a few years prior. She was now a fairly accomplished artist. I learned less about her brother but was impressed with how polite he was. Monika and I vowed to keep in touch.

A month after my arrival in Italy, I started to get antsy. John was supposed to be arriving soon by boat. In my spare time, I would sit on my bed and watch yachts entering Portofino's harbor, waiting for him to come. John had three yachts painted in battleship gray and named after Native American chiefs. When I saw the distinctive color emerge in the harbor, I grabbed my moped and headed down to meet him. My bright

---

2. For more information, see "L'Altra Dolce Vita" or the club's current website "Covo di Nord-est."

orange moped must've stood out as much as his battleship gray yacht, or perhaps it was my lanky, bronze-hued figure that caught his attention. Whatever it was, John was waving to me from the bow of his boat as I rounded the corner and approached the dock. As I was parking, he snuck up on me and gave me a warm, soul-stirring hug. The anticipation of seeing him again melted as he silently rocked me back and forth for a minute. Then he looked at me with his trademark wide grin and asked me to recount all I had been up to for the past month.

I spent the whole summer deejaying to save up money but relished my free time when I could hang out with John and his friends. I didn't think much of it at the time, but there was an unnamed tension that held our relationship together. People would often ask me what was going on between us. Little did they know that at that point in my life, I couldn't contemplate a loving relationship with anyone, even though it was love—all types of love—that I craved more than anything in the world, except for maybe my freedom. What I did know was that the love that I needed from John was different from the lust and desire that people around him trafficked in. What they assumed I got from him was not what he actually gave me.

Romantic love is only nourishing if you have fertile ground to plant it in. The events of my childhood had left nothing but scorched earth. The damage was not just from watching the fallout of my stepfather's abuse. It was also from surviving a world void of maternal guidance and care. While Zonnetta was so tender with her garden—so methodical in how she doled out love to her plants—her neglect and outright contempt for me ensured that any feelings I cultivated emerged stunted and malformed. It would be years before I was open to love or even physical affection, but I do credit John with being someone who showed me that love was possible. Through him, I learned what unconditional love was, something that people in healthy family environments begin learning at birth.

It was the summer of '69, and while the elite of Europe were vacationing on their yachts in blissful oblivion, the outside world was raging on. In New York, the Stonewall Riots ignited in June after yet another gay bar was raided by the police. After years of state violence, its victims finally revolted. The six-day uprising was the catalyst for decades of LGBTQ+ activism. Meanwhile, Vietnam war protestors and activists calling on equal rights for Black Americans continued their efforts. Both movements coalesced most succinctly in July, when Mohammed Ali was convicted of draft-dodging after refusing to kill brown people abroad for a country that treated its own Black and brown citizens worse than dogs. However, what stands out in my memory are not these historic events, but because after twenty-five years on this earth I got to celebrate my birthday for the first time in my life.

I don't think that I realized what I had been missing until I had experienced my first birthday party. For what it's worth, Mama always made sure to send me a gift for that special day. If it wasn't for her kindness, I probably would have never realized when my birthday was. No one else in my family ever mentioned it. Not even a "Happy Birthday." And with a summer birthday, I couldn't even rely on classmates at school to take note. The notion of a birthday party was not in my lexicon.

I can't remember when John learned this about me. It must've come up out of nowhere in some conversation of ours. If he had been shocked by the revelation that I'd never celebrated, he didn't share his reaction with me. As always, his face was set in that affable grin of his. When it rolled around that summer, I spent it as I did every birthday since my escape from Kansas: I wondered what my grandmother was up to. I tried not to think about family too often, but she always popped into my head on my birthday because she was the only one who had ever seemed to care about that day.

That evening, John picked me up and asked if I was hungry. I don't recall what my response was, but I was happy to arrive at my boss, Peppo Vanini's, restaurant. Peppo greeted me enthusiastically, like he greeted everyone, with a kiss on each cheek and then he opened the doors for me. At that moment, what seemed like hundreds of people jumped out of their seats and shouted "Tanti auguri!" as they threw confetti and sent balloons into the air. I don't remember any other details from that night. I just remember being consumed by an overwhelming feeling of joy and happiness. The world stood still, because for the first time in my life, someone was making it obvious to the world that I existed. I mattered.

When I wasn't working, I spent a lot of time on John's yacht. This was the first time that I had been on a boat. Before that, the only boat I had ever seen was a canoe. I still can't get over how huge it was. John constantly had guests aboard and usually most of them were beautiful, aspiring models. When it was time for lunch, John would drop anchor and call everyone to the top deck for lunch. One particular day, the chefs were serving lobster. I had never seen a lobster before, let alone eaten one. How often do lobsters come waltzing into Kansas? So here I was among a dozen or so bikini-clad, stunning women in their straw hats and a few equally gorgeous men. We were all asked to sit. John tried to put me near him, probably because he didn't know what I would do with a lobster in front of me and wanted to make sure I had some guidance, but I ended up getting pushed out to the margins as everyone grabbed a seat. The giant lobsters arrived at the table accompanied by utensils unfamiliar to me. I observed people squeezing plier-like tools to break the shell and scoop out the meat. Once I thought I understood how to use them, I put the plier around the claw of my lobster, and the whole thing went flying. Pieces of lobster went airborne in multiple directions. Mad hysteria broke out and I ran below deck in embarrassment. There was nowhere to hide.

Moments like these brought home how precarious my belonging was in these spaces. I was there because John wanted me to be there, but I didn't know what I was doing. My time in Los Angeles gave me a false sense of security that I was no longer a country bumpkin, but whenever I was placed in new situations, I fumbled over protocol. People stifled their ridicule because John wouldn't allow it, but the way that they would look at me and sneer was a constant reminder that my presence was simply tolerated. I was not born into this world of affluence, but I was adamant that I was going to exist in it with my pride intact all the same.

However, sometimes playing the part instead of recognizing one's limitations could be dangerous. On another glorious, summer day, I was on a Riva speedboat with John, his friend Antonio and a bunch of young women. I should've been in the middle with a life vest on since I couldn't swim. I was, instead, on the back with my big hat, tiny bikini, crossed legs and fierce expression, basically trying to be like the blondes who adorned John's boat. Antonio was steering and pointedly looked back at me. I figured out afterward that look was the sign to brace for a wave. The last thing I remember was seeing the front of the boat go almost vertical before I was thrown off the back. As I frantically tried to stay afloat, the boat plunged head-on into a couple more waves. Finally, they realized I was no longer with them. John took the wheel and steered the boat back around while Antonio jumped in after me. I kept bobbing under the water and when I went down a third time, Antonio somehow pulled me up to the lip of the boat. After dragging me back on board, they made a space for me to lie down. Miraculously, I had swallowed no water. As I was prostrate with everyone fussing over me, I just closed my eyes and thanked the sea. You don't play with the sea. When I opened them again, I saw a furtive tear wind down John's face. He later pulled me aside and said, "Venus, I thought I had lost you." While I never got used to nicknames and I hated people not calling me Alvenia, I made an exception for him because his nickname was the only one that I ever felt was a part of me. When he called me Venus, I knew he was talking to my soul. I promised that he would never lose me.

With a new appreciation for life but also a growing sense that I needed to rethink what actually brought me joy, I started to realize that I wanted to accomplish more in my life. As the club scene died down with the waning summer, I decided to make Geneva my base. Because of its international stature, I ran into people of different nationalities all the time and could hear about far-off lands. For the moment, I ignored the fact that Geneva was a little too sterile and clean for me. I started hanging out in cafés, especially in the university district, calmly drinking coffee and people-watching. As the weather started to get colder, these cafés offered nice respite from the chilly air.

One day, Pierre-Gilles Vidoli, a photographer from Geneva, came up to me as I thumbed through a fashion magazine between bites of an almond croissant. He opened with some line about how I could grace the pages of magazines like that. I told him that being a model had crossed my mind but that I didn't know where to start. Besides could someone like me actually be a model? There was nothing exceptional about me. He shrugged off my doubts and asked if I would join him for a walk to visit the office of a Jamaican woman named Maggie, who owned a small modeling agency called Agence One. She seemed excited to meet me. She then arranged for Pierre-Gilles to photograph me and set out to find me work.

I didn't think anything would come out of this endeavor. I had flirted with the idea of modeling and glamorous professions before but with little luck. When I was living in Los Angeles, one photographer told me that unless I bought a new nose, I wouldn't make it in the business. I did a lot of research and found a doctor known for nose jobs. I had saved up money and when I met the doctor at his fancy office on Wilshire Blvd., I explained how I wanted a nose like Sofia Loren's. That's who I flashed on when I thought about the perfect nose. He was sitting across from me in a large leather chair as I spread out all my magazine clippings on the table. As I rambled on about the perfect nose, he sat back and sighed before asking, "And do you also want me to take two inches from your arms?" He then continued to make fun of my request before ending with "Please, young lady, get out of my office."

I was taken aback at first. Wasn't this the profession he had chosen? Didn't he make a living off women's insecurities? But I began to look at that exchange as a blessing. He wasn't thinking about money. He was imagining a slippery slope where I would change everything about me into something I was not. I realized that as a Black woman in the sixties, I would have to change so much of myself to fit someone else's standard of beauty. If I gave one inch of myself then, I would eventually be left with nothing. Through his appalling rudeness, this doctor, a stranger who knew nothing about me or my attitudes about my body, let me feel okay about my nose. He was one of those people that the Spirit deemed necessary to put in my path. Over the years, I began to love that nose—the nose of my unknown father.

As I worked with Agence One, I also wondered if I had the stamina to be a model. Also, while in Los Angeles, I had tried out to be a Playboy bunny. I once met with retired bunnies called bunny mothers who ran an orientation for women who wanted to become bunnies. They helped you to put on the corset, high-heel shoes, and ears. They set up a table and showed you how to serve. You had to master the bunny dip with a drink on the tray. Every time I tried, I dropped the drink. They were very nice when they told me that I probably didn't have a career as a bunny.

However, working with Maggie turned out to be a low-stakes endeavor. I was usually called to be a pretty face at fancy parties in Italy. I never understood the mindset, but people loved to sprinkle us models among the invited guests. At one point, I was on assignment in Milan. I lived in a pensione with a whole bunch of other models and we would often be called upon en masse to attend these events. For one party in particular, we were to go to a village outside of Milan. A caravan of cars picked us up from our place to transport us to a lake where we were then escorted into little rowboats that took us to a castle on an island. All the other girls acted like attending parties in island castles was a normal occurrence.

We entered and encountered sheer opulence. There were long hallways with large, marble statues, as well as expensive paintings hanging on the walls. Lavish trays of exquisite hors d'oeuvres lined banquet tables. You could roam anywhere you liked. I went in search of a room with music, but to no avail. With all the care given to throwing a party, how could no one think to put on music? The grandeur of the place began to wear off and I started to get bored talking to rich people about mundane things. All of a sudden, there was raucous laughter and screaming emanating from down one of the long hallways. To everyone's amusement, Count Carlo Borromeo, the castle's owner, made a grand entrance by rolling through the castle on roller skates. Carlo was an eccentric gentleman, a descendent of a sixteenth-century Archbishop of Milan who shared the same name. I don't know what sort of expectations other people have for counts, but he definitely didn't fit mine.

I spent quite a bit of time in Italy during the fall, both for modeling gigs and for tourism. Besides the food, I loved Italy for the confidence it gave me. As much as I wanted to pretend that race didn't exist ever since I climbed up that tree in Kansas and asked God to rid me of racial karma, I was still always cognizant of being the only Black model; however, the way people received me in Italy made me sometimes think that being different didn't matter. I was blown away by how much Italians loved life. Everybody was beautiful there—young, old, fat, thin—because they were so happy to be alive. I distinctly remember a visit to Rome. I was walking down the Spanish Steps and two guys sitting there yelled out, "Bella donna" as I passed. It wasn't in a disrespectful way. They were just appreciating my beauty. It made me feel so good when for so much of my life, comments on the street were meant to make me feel bad.

As winter approached, I found myself spending more time in Switzerland. People just didn't need models when everyone was too cold to leave their homes. At some point, John asked me what I wanted to do for Christmas and I made up my mind that I was going to North Africa. Something drew me to Africa, and I was saving up my modelling money to afford airfare.

A few weeks before Christmas, John told me to hold off on buying the ticket. He had decided that he was going to Morocco with his wife for the holidays and was taking me with them. I learned that John had his own jet, a crimson Learjet called Chief Sloopy, which he piloted himself. The first time that I rode in his jet, I screamed because he hit Mach speeds soon after takeoff. He told me not to scream, but each time he did it, I would. It's something I could never get used to but that I found so exhilarating.

When we landed at a little airstrip outside Marrakech, the whole city seemed devoid of light. We stayed at a very traditional-looking palace with intricate geometric designs in the ceramic and woodwork. After dropping our bags, we went to a restaurant where we sat on cushions on the floor and ate tagine and couscous out of clay pots. I started hearing music through the floor and perked up. When I asked where it was coming from, no one else seemed to know what I was talking about. I excused myself and followed the music down a curvy staircase until I came across an older woman in a beautifully embroidered smock pounding peppers with a mortar and pestle. She was the music maker. I was so entranced by the sound emanating from the mortar that I just watched her for several minutes.

John, his wife, and I spent a few days exploring the whole city, winding through the narrow alleys and catching viewpoints of both the distant mountains and the courtyard gardens from the flat roofs that sheltered all the buildings. The holiday was soon over because John had to return to Geneva for business. I told him that I needed to stay longer. I wasn't ready to relinquish the dream of traveling around far-off lands. He asked if our tour guide would be willing to keep showing me around. I thus spent the rest of my trip as a guest in the tour guide's home, where I passed hours laughing with his family and breaking bread. Even though he was the only person I could communicate with through words, my interactions with all his family helped me understand this part of Morocco, little by little. The experience solidified my desire to see more of the world and put my return to Switzerland in a new light.

By 1970, I felt and acted like a local in Switzerland. I spent part of the winter in the Swiss Alps, marveling at the Matterhorn from the Zermatt Valley and once everything began to thaw out, I started studying fashion in Zurich, visiting John on weekends. John had given me access to the world, but once I was there, I didn't have to rely on him too much. He had his life and I had mine. I took the train all over Switzerland and through the surrounding countries, exploring large cities and small villages alike. I wanted to see the world and how people lived. I was still taking jobs through Agence One, with calls ramping up with the start of spring. I then resumed my deejaying at Il Covo for one last summer.

When I returned to Switzerland in September, I began to feel that it was a little small for me, the life a little too slow. My internal compass was spinning out of control and I needed to be on the move. I also realized that being in close proximity to John caused too much heartache. After a year or so of convincing myself otherwise, I finally admitted to myself that I was in love with John. He was so kind and generous, even if all people wanted to do was take, take, take. He didn't mind, though, because giving to others was what made him happy. He just loved life and had the wherewithal to enjoy it in such a gracious way. In many ways, I benefitted from John, as well, especially as it would've taken me much longer to achieve my dream of seeing the world without his beneficence; however, the true value of our friendship differed from what other people valued from him. While he gave me access to chic parties and fine dining, I didn't need any of that. In fact, it usually made me uncomfortable. I would've been just as content sitting in a garbage dump if it meant I could interact with John. Instead, his greatest gift was to break the barrier that I had with men. My childhood was defined by a father who I didn't know and a stepfather who stripped the humanity from my siblings and me. John allowed me to grow by seeing that there were other types of human interactions—ones based in love and respect—and I trusted him with my soul.

But I also knew that John wasn't mine. It was better for me to move on, having learned so much about myself and the world, than to grasp at something that would eventually lead to anguish. Maggie from the modeling agency told me of an opportunity in London where I could get signed with her sister company. I contacted my former New York neighbor Pat Hartley to let her know of my upcoming trip and I set it up to rent a room from them at 18 Elvaston Place. I said my goodbyes to John, thanking him for all he had done for me. He hugged me and whispered, "Venus, the world is yours."

Chapter 4: Jimi Hendrix in London

*Fig. 6. Jimi Hendrix memorial Greenwood Memorial Park,
Renton, WA. By Maya Angela Smith.*

Fig. 7. Alvenia holding the back cover of album Black-Man's Burdon. By Maya Angela Smith.

My parents moved to Renton, WA, in the middle of the COVID-19 pandemic to be closer to their first grandchild. One late afternoon, as I explored their new neighborhood, I stumbled across Greenwood Memorial

Park and found myself gravitating toward the stone dome in the distance. As I approached, I first noticed a marble sundial. While the overcast skies rendered it useless for telling time, it pointed to something more important: that greatness was buried just a few yards in front of me. My gaze soon met a giant metal guitar adorned with roses, perched on top of a grave marker that read "Forever in our hearts. James M. "Jimi" Hendrix. 1942 - 1970." Three stelae encircled the shrine, each with discolored black and white images of Hendrix. The discoloration first appeared to be a consequence of the drizzly climate, until I started to discern lip marks. Various shades of faded red—maroon, vermillion, burgundy, mahogany, rust, crimson—splotched his face. How many mouths had come to pay their respects? The image gave way to flowy lettering, beseeching the world to hear his message—a plea for love.

A few weeks later, I sat in Alvenia's living room teeming with excitement as I showed her the photographs that I had taken of Jimi's memorial (Fig. 6). When I got to a close-up of his lipstick-streaked face, Alvenia gave an audible gasp. Just like all the photos throughout her home, each marked with her daily salutations, this monument was a visual reminder of what certain people mean to others. As I read Jimi's words out loud, Alvenia repeated what she had told me hundreds of times before: "Jimi was a messenger."

*The second photo (Fig. 7) is of Alvenia holding a CD case that I came across while looking through her memorabilia. As always, she would not offer me any information unless I asked her outright. She seemed to enjoy sitting back and watching me try to piece together her life. I didn't recognize the album—*Black-Man's Burdon *by* Eric Burdon and War—*but the image of the woman who dominated the frame bore a striking resemblance to Alvenia. I studied her features. It was hard to know what this woman* *was thinking since a portion of her face was eclipsed by a bright orb, which added to her ephemeral presence. But something about this woman's stare unsettled me. A moment later, it hit me and as I peered over the album cover to seek confirmation, Alvenia pursed her lips and nodded slightly. So she was the woman in the photograph! She gingerly grabbed the CD case and said to me, "You may want to be sitting down for this story."*

I arrived in London at the beginning of September 1970 and met Pat Hartley and Dick Fontaine at their home on Elvaston Place. Pat was as spirited as always and it was great to see her and catch up about the last year and a half. After showing me my room, she introduced me to my new housemates. Pat and Dick were leaving soon to film a documentary in Hawaii and wanted to make sure I was well acquainted with everyone and everything before they left.

They had a big, terraced house divided so individual people could rent rooms and have autonomy. I had a room upstairs. We first stopped by the room of Amanda Lear, who Pat introduced to me as a "sex changeling."[1] While I had never heard that term before, even the brief period in New York City the previous year was enough to open my mind to the myriad ways people expressed gender and sexual orientation. Someone like her would've been ridiculed and possibly harmed if they walked down the street in Kansas, but in London, Amanda could become a famous model. Her close friendship with Salvador Dalí helped propel her fame, as she was his biggest muse. Amanda and I ended up working at the same modeling agency for a bit. She was very kind and made me feel right at home. Pat and I then stopped by the rooms of Graham Bell, a musician,

---

1. Lear's gender identity has been publicly debated.

and Andrew Coleman, a journalist—neither of whom I saw much of during my stay at Elvaston Place. Finally, Pat introduced me to my final flat mate, Judy Wong, an Anglophile from Sacramento who loved to follow British bands on the road.

I started my stint in London by stopping by the modeling agency to introduce myself. They put my name on the board and just like in Italy, gave me assignments that primarily involved my looking cute at rich folks' parties. It seemed that I was just pretty enough. My arms and legs, which had caused Zonnetta to relentlessly call me an Orangutan all those years, were seen as striking in the modeling world. Yet, no matter how glamourous I dressed or how well I mimicked the affectations of a model, my facial features were just not delicate enough to pass. The photographers and magazine editors in London were just as unimaginative as that photographer back in Los Angeles who had urged me to get a nose job. Besides, there were more Black women on the London scene and for any given event or shoot, an unwritten rule stated that Black models needed to remain a novelty and nothing more. You never saw more than one of us at a time. My frustration at realizing the modeling agency's lack of interest in me put somewhat of a damper on my experience in London, so I focused on finding spaces where I could enjoy myself and just be me.

I naturally gravitated to The Speakeasy on Margaret Street, just a couple miles away from Pat and Dick's. The place was always teeming with record producers and other people from the industry keen on catching the next global sensation. Unknown bands would play there for almost nothing, banking on their big break. Struggling musicians also relished the possibility of hanging out with some of the biggest names on the British Rock scene. Some members of the Beatles (who were in the process of breaking up by the time I arrived in England), the Rolling

Stones, and Led Zeppelin were just a few of the big acts that frequently jammed there. The space itself was quite small. There was a room where people would lounge, eating and chatting. The dance floor was outside and that's where I spent most of my time. I met Eric Burdon there and began spending some of my nights over at his place in sort of a free, unattached way.

Eric was from England but had spent a lot of time in the States. He had recently returned from San Francisco where he recorded an album with the funk rock band War. Eric and War were performing most nights around town and working on their next album. I enjoyed listening to his bluesy, soulful voice and spending time with a musician helped me quickly learn how to navigate London. No one was more adept at mastering a city than a musician because they were constantly seeking out the hot spots for music and merriment.

My interactions with Eric were short-lived and superficial, however. I still thought about John most of the time, wondering if I had made the right decision to put distance between us. I also didn't behave the way that men assumed I would. Men expected models, particularly aspiring ones, to be loose and begging for attention, but I was always quite reserved and uninterested in the sexual aspect of these dalliances. Men who tried to date me would quickly lose interest. I figured they kept me around as long as they did—a few weeks or so—because to the outside world I seemed like the perfect catch with my model-like proportions and supposedly "exotic" skin tone. But I wasn't interested in any of that. I was just starting to live, finally free and freedom meant traveling and experiencing the world.

A couple of weeks after my arrival, Pat and Dick went to Hawaii. Before leaving, they asked me to handle a few logistical issues related to the apartment. They had a friend who was going to stay in their room for a few days and instructed me to give him the key when he arrived. I was supposed to impress upon him the importance of not losing the key, because it was their only spare. They thought that he would arrive the following day or the one after, but they weren't sure of the time.

I called the agency to tell them not to book me those days. Pat and Dick made this guy's arrival seem really important, so I wanted to ensure that I was around to let him in. He didn't come the first day. By the evening, I thought about going dancing but dutifully stayed in to wait, having my first quiet night in a long time. The next day I waited around again, patient at first but growing slowly irritated as the hours ticked on. There were only so many times that I could read the magazines that I had picked up at the corner stand. By six p.m., I was feeling incredibly feisty because there hadn't been so much as a phone call. Finally, the doorbell rang. I opened the door and blurted, "You're late!" to the person standing there in a black hat that covered most of his face, before turning on my heels and walking several paces down the hall. However, my conscience started to get the better of me and I returned to the somewhat mystified man to apologize, "I'm sorry. That was very rude of me. I'm Alvenia. You can put your things down there." I pointed to Pat and Dick's room, the first on the left with the ornate double French doors, where he could deposit his bag and guitar.

"I'm sorry too, so let's not be sorry. I'm Jimi. It's a pleasure to meet you, Alvenia." He came across as so sweet and sensitive that I felt even worse about my initial treatment of him. I decided that I would let him relax and freshen up and then show him around the neighborhood. I pointed out the local pub and explained the lay of the land so that he wouldn't have any problem finding his way back to the apartment.

However, it turned out that he had been to London on multiple occasions, so he had a better sense of the city than I did. The whole time we were talking, he looked so familiar to me and then it hit me: he often hung out at the Scene in New York. While we had never actually met, we must've been in proximity on multiple occasions. He mentioned in passing that he was a musician, but at that moment I didn't realize how famous he was. I was just starting to get into Rock and Roll, with my friendship with Eric Burdon helping me learn about the genre. Jimi also never made a big deal of his stature in the industry.

After showing him around, I invited him to go with me to The Speakeasy, my favorite hangout spot, but he said that he had some things he needed to do first and would perhaps see me there. I was hoping to meet up with Monika Dannemann, who had started renting an apartment at the Samarkand hotel around the same time I arrived in London. We had become fast friends when I first met her at Il Covo di Nord-Est in Portofino. However, because she kept her own schedule hobnobbing with the world's elite and I was intent on making a break in the London modeling scene, we had been unable to connect. That morning, she had finally rung to tell me she'd be at The Speakeasy and was eager to see me.

I went back home for a bit because I never liked to go out dancing too early. When I got to The Speakeasy, Monika was sitting with her brother in the restaurant portion of the venue. As I joined them, I noticed Jimi across the way hanging out with Eric Clapton and The Speakeasy's usual suspects. Jimi looked over and waved at us and then went back to his discussion. I asked Monika if she wanted to meet Jimi.

She snorted at my naïveté. "Everyone knows Jimi Hendrix." She then let me know that the two of them had been an item ever since one of his concerts in Dusseldorf. I was reminded at that moment just how unhip I was when it came to the Rock and Roll world. While everyone was fawning over Jimi, the famous musician, I was thinking about Jimi, the young man who seemed so wistful when I met him. As Monika proceeded to tell everyone how amazing he was and how lucky she was to be his, I felt a little out of place and decided to do what I always did when I needed to think: I went to the dance floor. After a night of dancing, I bid farewell to Monika, who by this time was cozying up to Jimi on one of the couches.

A day or so later, I went to see Eric Burdon perform with War at a jazz club in Soho. Halfway through the set, Eric introduced Jimi as he got on stage. While the crowd went wild at first, their excitement dissipated a bit by the second song. I was mesmerized, watching the talent roll off his fingers with each pluck of the guitar, but I overheard someone next to me say how lackluster his performance was. Looking back, I can't help but think how sad it was for his star to go out with a whimper instead of as a blazing fire. No one in that room knew that it would be the last time they would hear Jimi Hendrix live.

The next morning, I was at Eric's, never suspecting that a frantic phone call would upend my life and the world of music in a split second. Mid-morning, Eric received a call, but it was for me. Apparently, Monika had telephoned Elvaston Place looking for me and Judy Wong had passed along Eric's number because she knew that I would be at his place. Monika was in a panic, repeating that she couldn't wake Jimi up. I didn't know what that meant. Eric, who was listening with me, took the phone. "You should call an ambulance. Now!" Then Monika hung up.

Eric turned to me. "You need to go over and check on everything. I'll call some of his people and see what I can do to help."

I hopped in a cab and headed to Notting Hill. Once at Monika's, I noticed that all the doors were open, which seemed odd. Telling the cab driver to wait, I ran into her apartment, but couldn't find anyone anywhere. I ran back to the cab and asked if he could take me to the nearest hospital. As we rolled up to St. Mary Abbot's, I found Monika sitting outside looking despondent. Her disheveled platinum hair had grown considerably since I had met her in Portofino. It now reached her waist. She was clutching Jimi's guitar case, rocking back and forth as she cradled it. I called out to Monika and even though I was only a couple feet away, she didn't respond. I grabbed her by the shoulders and gently shook her. She didn't acknowledge me other than to say, "Jimi's in there." I ran toward the medical staff and told them I was looking for my brother. They told me that I would have to wait.

I don't know why I referred to him as my brother at that moment. In my quick thinking, I must have thought that it would increase the likelihood of them giving me information. Besides, we were in an affluent part of London not frequented by Black people. It seemed plausible that we could be related. But when I really think about it, those words came so easy to me because even though I didn't know him well, I felt an instant and deep connection to him. It's something I've never been able to explain.

I repeated frantically, "Please, I need to find my brother. He's Black, in his twenties. I have to see my brother." At that moment, a doctor came out of one of the rooms down the nearest corridor to say to the nurse at the front desk that there was nothing they could do for their patient. He was gone. I wasn't sure if they were referring to Jimi but something in my gut knew it had to be him. "Are you talking about my brother? I need to see my brother!" I started screaming. I just went crazy to the point that they had to hold me down. They asked me to compose myself. I repeated again more calmly that I really needed to see him and pleaded that they escort me to wherever he was. They finally took pity on me and let me say goodbye. At this point, no one knew who this man was. Monika had hidden his identification because she thought there would be a media circus outside the hospital if anyone knew who he was. To the hospital staff, he was just another young man who had fallen victim to the vices of the party scene.

I will never forget that moment in his room. It was my first time witnessing death. Everyone has known someone who died, but this knowledge cannot prepare you for the emotions that come when a life is extinguished too soon. If they hadn't told me that he was dead, I wouldn't have believed it. He looked as if he were asleep, finding the peace in death that he couldn't find in life. He had his arms crossed over his body with his turquoise ring still adorning his finger. My tears were my offering to the Spirit to grant him safe passage to whatever came after death. At this point in my life, I did not have a well formulated philosophy on the existence of a higher power, but talking with Jimi had a profound effect on me. Only something like the Spirit could've created a person such as this and allowed me, a nobody, to cross paths with him. While I had only known him for a few days, I was convinced that he was a messenger who was put on this world to share a transcendent gift.

Suddenly, one of the nurses asked me to fill out paperwork. They needed information on who he was. I told them to give me a minute. I needed to make a phone call. I went to one of those red telephone booths and fumbled through my pocket for the number of Eric Barrett, Jimi's road manager and right-hand guy. Eric Burdon had given me his number before I left his place. When Eric Barrett picked up the phone, I explained who I was and how I was at St. Mary Abbot's hospital and that Jimi was gone.

"What do you mean, gone?"

I replied numbly, "Jimi is dead."

"Where are you again?" he asked with a tone laced with irritation. I repeated how I was at the hospital, and before I finished explaining where it was, he said, "Get the fuck out of there," and hung up the phone.

Up until that moment, I had only been thinking about Jimi. Eric Barrett's command ripped me momentarily from my state of mourning. I knew I had to get Monika out of there. I found Monika where I had first seen her. She was on a bench outside, still looking catatonic. I grabbed Monika's hand and willed her to come with me. "Monika, we have to get out of here. Once people know it's Jimi, there will be chaos."

Monika nodded but didn't say a word. She was still clutching his guitar.

We slipped out of the hospital when the woman who had asked for Jimi's information wasn't looking. I felt like I was abandoning Jimi but the tone in his manager's voice and his forceful command were too powerful to ignore. I grabbed a cab and said the address of the first place that came to mind: Eric Burdon's hotel. He had planned to shoot the cover of his latest album that day and so I instinctively went to the roof to find him. I opened the door and saw Eric sitting on the roof's edge with the skyline behind him. When Eric looked up and saw me with a despondent Monika, I could tell that he knew. I sat Monika down on one of the chairs as he told the photographers to get out.

I walked over to him and settled in for a long embrace. I told him that I needed to sit down and turned around right there to sit on the ledge. I then took a moment to relish the fresh air circulating so high up. It felt much cleaner than the air at street level. I was finally able to exhale. It felt like I hadn't breathed since I got that fateful call.

As reality started sinking in, I noticed that one of the photographers had returned. He approached us and said, "Please, just keep sitting as you are. Eric, stand between her and sort of slouch down with your back against the wall. Now grab her ankles." I was sort of aware of what was happening but too emotionally drained to make any decisions for myself. I just listened to the photographer's cues. Eric nestled his head between my open legs and stared at the camera. I heard the click and an exclamation of delight from the photographer and that was that. Amidst my grief and heartache, the back cover of the album *Black-Man's Burdon* was created.

At that point, Eric definitely kicked everyone out and said the session was over. We went over to Monika, who had finally emerged from her catatonic state and had begun crying. Eric turned to Monika and said he would take her to her apartment. He prepared her for the fact that there could be police wanting to investigate and that she may need to make a statement. He then turned to me and said, "Listen, Alvenia, you shouldn't go back to Elvaston Place. You and Monika should come with me to Newcastle." Eric was about to go on the road with his band so that they could promote their music. Originally, I had said no when he offered to take me on the road, but at this point, it seemed like a good way to get out of London and away from the epicenter of this nightmare.

The next few days were a complete blur. I remember boarding a train to Newcastle at some point. I had nothing with me but my ID and the clothes on my back. That dress, the one that was captured on the back cover of the album, was what I was wearing when I saw Jimi for the last time. I don't know how many days I wore it until I got a change of clothes. Whenever I see that album, I relive that moment—that awful moment—when I said goodbye to Jimi.

It didn't take long for the press to catch wind of Jimi's death and salivate over the uncertainty about what happened in those last hours. They weaved together all sorts of tales as they tried to arrange the pieces. Neither Monika nor I could sleep. Monika had always been an insomniac, relying on the same German sleeping pills that had contributed to Jimi's death, but she no longer had them with her and was running on fumes. I tried to talk to her about what had happened, but she was so delirious and sleep deprived that I couldn't make sense of the sequence of events. She just kept repeating that he vomited in his sleep and was choking. I learned later through the newspapers that he died of asphyxia. His system was full of barbiturates from Monika's sleeping pills. At some point during the days after Jimi's death she muttered how she wished she had known to turn him over. She blamed herself for not knowing what to do when she found him unresponsive.[2]

I don't know how I separated from Monika and barely remember returning to Switzerland. It took weeks before I emerged from a waking dream. Throughout the years, though, Monika has haunted me. By the time I was living in New York again, she would come every year. Each time, she begged and begged me to move to Germany. I watched her slowly lose her grip on reality as she descended head-on into a legal battle with one of Jimi's other girlfriends, Kathy Etchingham. No one could convince Monika to let go of the past. She was an incredible painter and spent the rest of her life devoting her artistic talent to enshrining Jimi in

2. Much speculation has circulated around Hendrix's death. See Hendrix & McDermott, *Jimi Hendrix*, and Shapiro and Glebbeek, *Jimi Hendrix*.

this medium. She always wore the same purple dress, the one she had on when she met Jimi. She had someone sew a whole wardrobe of identical dresses, which she wore religiously. It was as if she were stuck in one of her paintings. She came from a very wealthy industrial family and her parents even tried to convince me to move to Dusseldorf in order to help her move on. They were prepared to pay for all my expenses and accommodation in hopes that I could ground her in a reality that didn't involve worshipping Jimi. But I didn't know what I could do for her. She was living solely for him.

She eventually moved to England and married a rock guitarist. However, from what I heard, she was still stuck in her past. The feud with Kathy continued for several decades and by 1996, she was found in contempt of court for saying various things about Kathy. At that moment, Monika gave up her will to live and committed suicide by gassing herself with the exhaust fumes in her car. She had always been a fragile person and she didn't have the strength to fight the memory of Jimi, the disdain from a public who thought she bore some responsibility in his death, an unending and contentious feud with Kathy and a legal system that she deemed unfair.

I also had my difficulties in letting go. Jimi had been in my life for such a short period of time, but it was the most life-changing of experiences. Over a decade after Jimi died, Alan Douglas, the American record producer who had spoken with Jimi a few days before his death and who in some ways became Jimi's posthumous manager by controversially reworking Jimi's recordings and releasing them, approached me to be a consultant for the Jimi Hendrix Foundation. We did things like put on an art show where various artists painted portraits of Jimi. I wasn't surprised that the line of people went around the block to get into the Soho gallery we rented in New York. Jimi had touched so many. However, one day I realized that while I wasn't as entranced as Monika, I was in some way living my life for Jimi as well. I found that my honoring him was bordering on fanaticism. I gave away most of my Jimi memorabilia, only keeping a blown-up color photocopy of a smiling twelve-year-old Jimi outside his home in Seattle and a black and white photo of him sitting at an airport with angel wings drawn directly on the photo. Letting go of everything else helped me to let go of his death and start really celebrating his life.

Meanwhile, speculations surrounding Jimi's death continued to bubble. There were stories that swirled around about him being owned by his record label, the mafia, or both. No one could get a true handle on the timeline of events that led to his death. While it was clear how he died, it wasn't clear what circumstances allowed him to be in that predicament, so the coroner in 1970 recorded an open verdict. The case was reexamined in 1993 but found inconclusive once again. While the law will no longer try to figure out what led to the world losing one of its brightest stars, the stories surrounding his death will continue piquing the world's imagination for a long time to come. As for me, my consolation is my belief that Jimi was put here on this earth to inspire through music and inspire, he did.

Chapter 5: New York City in the Seventies

Fig. 8. Alvenia looking at a photo of herself in Scavullo. By
Maya Angela Smith.

Fig. 9. Signed photo of "Shoe Metamorphosis, Alvenia Bridges wearing Charles James," 1978. Pencil and watercolor on paper. © The Estate and Archive of Antonio Lopez and Juan Ramos. Used with permission.

When Alvenia first showed me the photograph by Francesco Scavullo from 1975 that had been reprinted in the book Scavullo *(Fig. 8), I was struck by her confidence. This woman was a far cry from the girl who had major complexes about her body. I once asked her what her complexes were and I'll never forget her gesticulations as she snorted, "My arms are as long as my legs. They are three feet long. I have no body!" Yet, she wields said body with such poised strength in this photo. Her unwavering stare arrests the viewer. She is completely at home in a scene in which she originally wasn't supposed to be present. While Jerry Hall occupies the central position, Alvenia takes up the most space. She is the one whose image lingers on your retinas long after you have shut the book.*

But Alvenia's ability to command attention does not stop with photography. The stylized portrait that Antonio Lopez drew of Alvenia in 1978 (Fig. 9) conjures up the same indomitable spirit captured in Scavullo's photograph and in the stories Alvenia tells about her life. The metamorphosis Antonio lays out on the page, mirrors the transformation Alvenia underwent in her own emergence as a woman coming into her own.

All the professional photos and images of Alvenia mesmerize the viewer. I find it surprising that she never became a household name in fashion. However, what is even more shocking is the fact that she was never paid for her labor. When I asked her why not, she simply responded that she never thought about money in those instances. She made it clear that unlike established models, her appearances in magazines and other venues were always by happenstance—such as fooling around with friends after a shoot. I still think that she gives herself too little credit and I wonder how many other women's work has gone unpaid and unrecognized.

For weeks after Jimi's death, I replayed the haunting image of his lifeless body, lying there on that cold slab. I tried to travel in order to claw my way out of this period of grief, but nothing gave me solace. Switzerland was no longer a haven. The novelty had worn off. Besides, I couldn't return to John. There were too many women vying for his affections, most of all his current wife. John, like my grandma, had opened the world for me, but it was time to move on. I made the decision to return to New York City.

It had been fun for a while, to play the part of the swanky European who vacationed on yachts and rubbed shoulders with the global elite, but an urge to return to my home country began to develop. Little did I know how hard this transition back to the States would be. My time in Europe allowed me to experience a world that wasn't constantly dictated by race. Granted, there were moments when I was reminded that I was an anomaly. My dark skin stood out, especially in the modeling world. But I also stood out because of my class background. I was not bred into the social echelons that I frequented when I was with people like John. I actually never truly belonged. Then again, I wasn't shunned either.

But as soon as I landed in the United States, I was reminded of how segregated the country was. I'm not talking about Kansas. That will forever be etched into my mind as the place where I failed to integrate at school or where people hidden behind robes could set your belongings on fire without consequences. But I had always thought that the coasts were different. My new European perspective made the differences between the coasts and the heartland less stark. When I landed at JFK, I started to remember racism. Not the violent, obvious forms, but the more insidious types woven into the fabric of society and permeating the very way that society is structured. For instance, I was taken aback by how all the porters were Black. All the busboys were Latino. Anyone in a position to serve was a person of color.

It dawned on me at that moment, that I had barely seen Black people when I was in Europe in the sixties. I was happy to escape the constant reminders of race and be in a place where I was not made to feel invisible for being Black. Because I was seen, I never even thought about my color while in Europe. But I also knew that my existence was tolerated because I was providing a service as an exotic adornment to spice up lavish parties. Don't get me wrong, I loved how most people treated me with respect and in a civilized manner, but I also understood that they did so because I played a very specific role. I loved Europe for the opportunities it allowed me, but I knew that, in a way, it could only offer me so much.

Contrary to the excitement I felt about traveling a new path when I first embarked on my return journey, I saw my enthusiasm drifting away each moment I witnessed the United States' rigid racial hierarchies. On the one hand, it was great to see so many beautiful people of color; on the other hand, our strength in numbers served to illustrate our social stratification where, like grains of sand, we settled to the bottom. However, New York City was probably one of the only places in the US where there was some space to subvert these restrictions. I had made my decision to throw myself into New York City life and regardless of what I encountered, I was there to stay.

The first thing I did, after seeing James Finney both to catch up and get my hair done, was find a job. While it was brief, my job at the Genesis on East 48th Street was probably a low point in my years of employment. After opening in 1970, the Genesis was the stomping ground of eccentric owner Rocky Aoki, the founder of Benihana, who had created this club mainly so that he could prey on hot women, snort cocaine and bet wild amounts of money on backgammon. The disco succeeded as a great place to live the playboy lifestyle but failed as a business venture—shuttering its doors after a year in operation. However, the name lived on with the founding of his pornographic magazine, *Genesis*, which still exists today.[1]

Other than being one of the sleaziest jobs that I ever had, Rocky had a strict dress code that conflicted with my true essence. I didn't mind the scantily clad requirement of the job. I had been in the modeling world long enough to know that that was how things worked. But I bristled at their insistence that I cover up my Finney plaits. They forced me to wear a wig. I hate wigs. It reminded me of my mother, whose platinum blond wigs were as unnatural as her parenting skills and her disdain for me. Before I encountered the stylish, thin plaits that James Finney bedecked my head with, I had spent a lifetime rocking four simple braids. These braids were something that I could do myself, giving me an independence that often does not accompany Black hair care. The only time I wore a different style was for the holidays, when Zonnetta insisted on hot combing my hair. I had to sit up straight on a wooden stool or risk getting wacked on the back with the comb. Once she finished, I wasn't allowed to play, because if I perspired, my hair would frizz out. Climbing

---

1. For more information, see Schlagenhauf, "Cocaine, Boats, and Backgammon."

up my favorite tree was out of the question. That hair style exerted a type of control over me that I resented.

Somebody else chose a new, required wig for me, since I was going to participate in this charade as little as possible. The wig was simple—brownish, straight hair to match my skin. But it wasn't me. When I wore Finney plaits, no one could mess with me. There was something regal about them. I have always believed that our hair is our crown. For them to deny me this, they must have thought that they could wrest away my power like that of the Biblical Sampson. Little did they know that my power came from inside. But their ignorance and their insistence on western forms of beauty did make me sad. They thought that by erasing parts of me, they could take away who I was. The disco shut down soon after it opened, but if it hadn't, I'm sure I would've quit.

I took a series of odd jobs throughout the early seventies to help support myself through school. While I had been gone from New York for a couple years, I had not forgotten my dream of going to the Fashion Institute of Technology (FIT). Fashion attracted me because I liked pretty clothes and pretty things. I was particularly interested in learning draping techniques, an important element in fashion design. I didn't know if I wanted to be a designer; I'd never thought that far ahead. I just thought that it would be interesting to work with some of the well-known Black designers such as Steven Burrows or Scott Barrie, or my idol, Haitian designer Fabrice Simon.

The monotony of working long hours to cover housing and school expenses was daunting, but life picked up once I started attending FIT and interacting with a variety of interesting people. Someone I literally crossed paths with was Antonio Lopez, the Puerto Rican fashion illustrator who grew up in New York City, but who split his time between there and Paris. When I met him, he was all bubble, just free and spirited with an infectious laugh.

I met Antonio at my most flustered as I tried to find my direction while at the corner of 56th and 7th. Most of my time was spent below 27th street. In looking for a modeling agency that was way out of my geographic comfort zone, I stopped a vibrant man and asked, "Excuse me, sir, could you direct me to the east?"

He donned this huge smile and explained in detail how to do the simple task of going east. He must've known that I had a wacky sense of direction when I was out of my element. Then he asked, "Would you be willing to pose for me?" He didn't even ask if I was a model.

I inquired, "Pose?" I had no idea what that meant, since all my small modeling gigs consisted of me standing around at different events, but I was wide open to anything and accepted his business card with excitement.

I went to my scheduled appointment but called Antonio immediately afterward and we set up a time for a few days later. His studio was in Carnegie Mews, next to all sorts of creative, artistic people. Bill Cunningham, who used to photograph for the *New York Times*, had a space there and there was a network of folks such as the model Pat Cleveland and various designers. To the shoot I took my current prized possession, a pair of Yves Saint Laurent three-inch heels. I wore tights under a pair of pants and a blouse. Nothing too flashy. I figured he would dress me in whatever he saw fit. When I came in, he outfitted me in a stunning, green, Charles James designer jacket and then showed me how and where he wanted me to stand. "Like a princess," he said, which meant I couldn't slouch. He had me put my arms behind my back in a sort of yoga stance, as if I was about to dance. Then he ordered—not in a commanding way because he was all smiles—to put my chest to the sky: "Sternum up, chin out."

I stood in that position for eight hours. It was excruciatingly painful to hold that form for so long, but I didn't dare break pose because he would get out of his element. It was the first and only time I did so, because I wasn't cut out for that type of modeling.

Antonio was able to see beauty in me, in a way that disinterested modeling agencies never did. He had the creativity to capture my essence and make me feel like a queen. He also said I was a perfect model because of my lack of booty. Designers could put me in anything. Years later, he gave me a signed copy of "Shoe Metamorphosis," which was replicated in *Antonio's Girls*. He had written, "For Alvenia, with all my love. Thanks a million." Regardless of the pain I felt standing there for all those hours, it is one of my favorite memories of that time of my life. Through his incredible artistry, he made me into a shoe. I would forever be one of Antonio's girls.

While my career as a model never really took off, my life intersected the international fashion world in numerous ways. I befriended some up-and-coming actresses and models such as Geraldine Smith, one of Warhol's superstars, and Winona Williams, a Wilhelmina model who dated both Paul McCartney and David Bowie. I have remained close friends with Geraldine until this day. But one of my closest friends—until we had a falling out—was Jerry Hall.

You would think that with someone as glitzy and glamorous as Jerry, we would have met under more extravagant circumstances. Instead, I found her weeping in the corner of Jonathan Hitchcock's empty show-room on 26th and 6th. While attending FIT, I worked as an intern for Jonathan, a well-known designer. He was a genius, but a real high-strung queen. He had sent me out to look for brass zippers, even though every-one else by that point had switched to plastic. I had been scouring the garment district to no avail and was afraid to go back to the showroom empty handed. I waited until I was sure that he would be gone and then returned to clean up, only to find Jerry there. Jonathan was friends with Antonio Lopez—who I wouldn't meet on that street corner for a couple more years—and Jerry had followed Antonio from Paris, where she had worked with him and had even been roommates. She was so in love with Antonio at the time, not realizing, or more accurately, not accepting, that he was gay. Besides her dating woes, she had just started modeling for Eileen Ford, but didn't want to stay with the other girls. She seemed in so much distress that I offered her a place in my little loft on Ann St. down by City Hall. I warned her that the floor was painted blue and that I didn't have any furniture other than one bed and a big butcher's table. At that point, that was good enough for her.

We stayed on Ann St. a while, but it didn't last long. "You're too far downtown," Jerry complained. "We have to move uptown." So, we moved up to 14th street, around Union Square. Jerry's modeling career was taking off, and I was continuing my work as a cocktail waitress in the evening and going to FIT during the day. We were just doing, being, growing and learning together and from that, a friendship blossomed.

We were so similar, yet so different. We were both six feet tall, but she had bone-straight, long, blond hair while I was rocking the Finney plaits.

We both entered the modeling world, but she would become one of the most recognizable names of her generation and I would wind up on a path away from the spotlight. We both came from small towns in the middle of the country, she from Mesquite, Texas to a close-knit family, and I from Kansas City, Kansas, where homelife could've one day been the literal death of me. She was obsessed with men and had no problem using them to advance her career, while I spent years working behind the scenes to help many men shine artistically with no expectation of anything in return. But at this point in our lives, we were close friends bound by more commonalities than differences.

Before she hit it big, we spent our time surviving in New York by not letting our lack of funds keep us from imagining a high-class lifestyle. One time, we didn't have any heat. Somewhere, there's a picture of us near freezing to death while sipping on champagne and indulging in caviar.

I remember what she said to me that night, "Beanie, I want a rich man, diamonds and furs."

I replied, "I simply want love and happiness." This exchange said a lot about her as well as our relationship. She insisted on calling me Beanie, even though the only nickname I ever accepted in my life was Venus. I repeatedly told her not to call me Beanie, which was a nonsensical name, but she did what she wanted. Her words also reflected what she truly believed. Her mother Marjorie had instilled in her that if she could secure a rich man, diamonds, and furs, then the world would be hers. Since making it big, she has never been without any of those things and perhaps she's happy.

In many ways, she was a well-meaning friend, but she was often so clueless as to how her actions affected those around her. A particularly traumatic experience was the year that she took me on a surprise vacation for my birthday. Having spent my childhood devoid of birthdays, any recognition meant a lot to me. When she told me to pack a bag for a warm climate, I thought we were going to Jamaica or somewhere tropical. She bought plane tickets for about five or six women and when we got to our gate, I saw the word "Dallas" on the board. I hoped it was just a layover, but no, our final destination was Mesquite, her hometown, a suburb of Dallas. I had never been to Texas before, but it was the seventies and I couldn't imagine that things were much better than the 1960s Kansas I had left and never looked back at.

I tried to have a positive attitude about the trip. At Dallas airport, I met her sister Cindy, who was a barrel racer and all-around cool gal. From this, I hoped that perhaps things would be okay. When all the girls and I pulled up into the driveway, Jerry's parents walked towards us.

As her father helped us out the cars, he turned to me, looked me up and down and said, "Why aren't you the prettiest n***** I've ever seen?" That moment left me stunned. I hadn't been directly called that since I had left Kansas. That was the word the KKK used when they would screech their tires outside our house. That was the word that those kids used as they hurled Coke bottles at my head. I had spent so much of my adult life escaping any memory of that word that when it slid off his tongue as smoothly as chewing tobacco sludge, I was unable to move. There was no way for me to respond to ignorance like that. It was as if he had put a hex on me.

I didn't want to spend much time in their house, but I was also wary about going out. There were some activities that I enjoyed, such as when we got to try our hand at horseback riding or when we swam in a river and someone pushed Geraldine off the bridge overhead to the delight of everyone swimming below. When it was just us girls and I was among friends, I could enjoy my birthday. Then there were other activities I should've enjoyed but couldn't. For instance, Jerry was excited to take me dancing because she knew how dancing was my life, but I was wary of meeting new people. If someone like her father could say such a vile thing to a guest in his home, what would people say to me in public? But what could I do? We piled into cars and arrived at a place where a bull sculpture about the size of a building guarded the entrance.

As we crossed the threshold, we entered a huge dance hall. Numerous cowboys and cowgirls adorned with hats and boots were dancing in a line. Jerry and her sisters were practically pushing me through the door. Jerry was so excited, because for them, they were giving me the biggest treat. But I could not get over my Texas welcome and thus found it hard to enjoy the evening. We sat at a long table covered in pitchers of beer. Various guys would come and ask all the other women at our table to dance and I just sat there watching. Jerry must have felt bad, because at some point, she came back with a cowboy in tow. As she introduced him to me, he took my hand and walked me to the dance floor. I made it a point to try to pick up the dance. I think it was called the two-step. Dancing is universal and it was my birthday, so I could at least put in an effort. But when he unceremoniously deposited me back at the table, all he said was "You got too much boogie in your pants." The whole weekend was one of the most excruciating experiences of my life.

At the same time, my relationship with Jerry offered me some fonder memories even if they were often borne of frustrating circumstances. One day back in New York, I was ready to kill Jerry because she hadn't left the house keys for me. I called her agency and learned that she was with Francesco Scavullo, a fashion photographer who was adept at creating amazing celebrity portraits. His studio was located between Park and Madison at that time. I'll never forget it because the walls were painted black. When I arrived, Jerry was in the middle of a photoshoot alongside Margaret Broderick. I spotted Scavullo's partner, Sean Byrnes, and asked if he could get my house keys from Jerry. All of a sudden, Jerry came out of the adjoining room, completely naked. As I explained to her how I needed the keys so I could get to my waitressing job, Scavullo waved and said, "Alvenia, come on in. You're just in time!" He proceeded to roll out a big black furball and instructed Jerry and Margaret to get behind it. Then, he turned to me and asked, "Would you like to join the shoot?"

I didn't know what I was doing, but that didn't matter. When I disrobed and placed myself by Jerry and behind the prop, I innately understood how to make myself fit into the scene. It all seemed so natural to me. The photo apparently came out in Italian *Vogue* later that year, but I wouldn't see it until a reprint years later, when my dear friend Nick Ashford came across it on a flight and lovingly teased me about it. I'll never forget his exclamation, "Alvenia, I never knew how well-endowed you were!"

As Jerry's career took off and she moved out, I began to see less and less of her. We wouldn't spend much time in proximity again until the early eighties, years after she started seeing Mick Jagger, when I became Mick's personal business liaison. However, Jerry and I did meet up from time to time while out and about. We were particularly known to bump into each other at Studio 54.

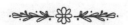

Just as the Whisky-a-Go-Go, the Scene and The Speakeasy had been the main venues of the day, Studio 54 was the current incarnation of the place to be. In 1977, Steve Rubell and Ian Schrager transformed a former theatre into the nightclub but kept some of the previous aesthetics. They hired a team of people who created mobile theatrical sets and unlike most discos, they could light up the dance floor when they wanted to create dramatic effects. The list of its regular patrons was populated with so many big names, that one could pretty much expect that there would be no space for "normal" people. I was surely a normal person, but early on I had befriended Steve and there always seemed to be a place for me. I never had to call ahead. I could simply show up and skip the line. Because I lived a block away, I would roll out of bed after a quick post-work nap and be there in no time. Besides, I was a loyal patron who was there nearly every night and only ever hung out on the dance floor, so it was as if I was part of the background.[2]

Although I was a staple, I missed out on everything that drew most people there. I just wanted to dance but people mainly went there to enjoy life's excesses. I found out later that all the hard drugs happened in the VIP section. There was no dance floor in the VIP section, so I never even thought about going there and that may have been my saving grace. I lost quite a few friends in that era—people who overdosed or who watched their careers slip through their fingers and even if they were one day able to get sober, they sometimes decided that suicide was easier than trying to pick up the pieces. Some people, like Jerry, were able to bypass the drug-fueled hedonism of the time. We both were much happier with a couple of glasses of wine than with debilitating

---

2. To get a sense of Studio 54's exclusivity, see Segell's "Studio 54."

benders. We also had similar spritely personalities and could make any situation fun. A photograph that Antonio Lopez shot of us hanging out of a phone booth in front of Studio 54 probably best captured our whimsical spirit, which was seldom impeded by outside forces. I could never understand altering my mind when it was already driving me crazy. Besides, I knew what could happen when I smoked pot. I wasn't willing to find out what effect harder drugs would have on me.

The Studio 54 years were like a whirlwind. Its meteoric rise was followed by a crash down to earth. The IRS became suspicious when they posted record profits without corresponding tax payments. Steve and Ian would soon go to jail, albeit briefly and while they both went on to other ventures after their release, Steve would only live a few more years. I was sad to learn that he passed away from AIDS-related complications. Like so many of that era, there was so much misinformation surrounding what would end up being a full-blown epidemic. Too many people would lose their lives not only to drugs but to horrific illness.

Somehow, I stayed above the fray. It was just me and New York City. I went with the flow, even though chaos swirled around me. Spinning around on the dance floor had become my forcefield, thus I floated through this harrowing period—my life on a path the direction of which was unknown. I resolved to rely on the Spirit to be my compass, trusting happenstance to light my way.

Part 2: People Make the World Go 'Round

Chapter 6: Roberta Flack and the Business of Showbusiness

Fig. 10. Alvenia staring at a signed photo of Roberta Flack with personalized note. Original by Dakotah. By Maya Angela Smith

Fig. 11. Alvenia displaying a photo of her with James Finney.
Original by unknown. By Maya Angela Smith.

Each morning, Alvenia greets those who have meant the most to her life with a kiss—her lipstick a lasting reminder of the homage she pays. Alvenia's lipstick is most visible on Roberta Flack's autographed black-and-white photo where Roberta refers to herself as Alvenia's godmother (Fig. 10). Indeed, Roberta has always used her power and influence to uplift others. Her patronage of Alvenia was no exception. She saw some-

thing in Alvenia and through her lofty expectations, she molded Alvenia into one of the best tour managers out there.

While Roberta was like a godmother to Alvenia, James Finney was her anchor and the bearer of firsts (Fig. 11). He was the person who first clued Alvenia in on the existence of cosmopolitan Blackness when they met in Los Angeles and the first who urged Alvenia to strike out on her own when he told her she belonged in New York. He was the first person she always contacted when she returned to New York after stints in Europe, and, by putting her in touch with Roberta, the person who orchestrated her career in music. Furthermore, Black womanhood ran all through her Finney plaits—the delicate braids that Finney lovingly created for her and by far her most important physical possession. Because of him, she learned to not be ashamed of her hair.

While Finney was Alvenia's anchor, Alvenia was his biggest champion. She would do whatever it took to make sure he was treated well. When he started to lose his battle with AIDS in the height of the epidemic, Alvenia was his rock—sometimes taking her role a little too enthusiastically. When she started berating the nurses assigned to him, because of what she saw as substandard care, Roberta stepped in, took over and limited Alvenia's visitation at the hospital. The specter of Finney's impending death was too much to bear, so Alvenia listened to Roberta and retreated. She said her final goodbye to Finney in 1993 by arranging his celebration of life service at his little church on 91st and Columbus. As laughter filled the pews while guests shared their favorite Finneyisms—funny phrases that Finney coined throughout his life and that Alvenia still uses today—Alvenia sat outside on the stoop, tears streaming down her face. She needed the warmth of the sun to get her through and thus decided to listen to the service from there.

In September 1979, I landed back in New York City after another vertiginous modeling stint in Europe. All those years ago, when Mama made me tell her my dream and gave me that globe to signal that she had heard my plea, I realized the power of putting my desires out into the universe. Nothing would change unless I prepped the world to help change things for me. I said to myself that I would tell anyone who listened that I was back, on the loose and looking for work.

I paid a visit to James Finney, the first person I contacted any time I returned to New York. As a hairstylist to some of the most famous Black performers of the era, he could possibly provide some guidance. Besides, I needed my hair done. To this day I have never let another person touch my hair. Having Finney do your hair was an experience. He performed magic with his fingertips. Through his work, he made women love themselves. People were so desperate to have Finney plaits, that they would put up with just about anything. Finney was a character like no other.

When you were in his care, you were not allowed to leave the chair, other than for bathroom breaks, no matter how long it took for him to complete his work. If Finney decided he wanted to go to the bar on the corner for a drink, he would tell you, "I'll be back, directly," and two hours could pass by before he would come sauntering back into his salon with a wide grin on his face. If he got hungry, he would go into the adjoining kitchen and fry himself a chicken. It didn't matter what stage he was at with your hair. It could wait. He would always offer you a choice piece of that bird in exchange for your patience. He also had a television on in every room. He didn't want to miss his soaps while he was working and his multiple-screen setup allowed him to move from room to room and still enjoy a seamless viewing experience.[1]

That particular morning, Finney was plaiting my hair and between long glances at *Days of our Lives* and listening to me lament about how fed up I was with fashion; he dexterously braided my hair so fine that each braid looked like a strand of hair. He swung his own plaits over his shoulder and cocked his head suddenly. "You know," he exhaled pensively, "I just might have a lead for you. Let me see what I can do."

A few days later, Roberta Flack, who was riding high after taking the music world by storm in the 1970s with hits such as "Where is the Love?" and "Killing Me Softly with his Song," was sitting in the exact same chair I had been and having the exact same style done.[2] Finney plaits were all the rage at this time. Always a reliable friend, Finney casually brought me up in conversation and related how I was looking for a career change.

"Is that right?" Roberta responded to his brief monologue. "Where's your phone? I might as well call her now since I still need a tour manager and it seems like she needs a job."

Finney dug out the phone from under a pile of curlers.

When the call came, I was combing over the classified ads in my tiny little studio apartment on West 55th Street. This funky little studio was so small, that if you walked through the door you would fall out the front window. But it was close to Central Park and to all the places I wanted to be in the city, so I didn't mind my closet of an apartment. None of the ads were jumping out at me, so I was starting to get a bit anxious about

---

1. The Schomberg Center in New York has a series of interviews where James Briggs Murray speaks with Finney about Black hair care.

2. For more about Roberta Flack, see the *American Masters* documentary about her life.

affording even this closet I called home. Answering the phone, I heard the voice on the other line say, "Alvenia Bridges?"

"Yes?"

"This is Roberta Flack."

I jumped and nearly fell backwards out that front window. Quickly gathering my wits, I replied, "Yes, Ms. Flack?"

"Roberta."

A layer of sweat had condensed on my upper lip. I noticed that my hand was slightly shaking, causing the phone to vibrate against my ear. Worried that too much time had passed with no response, I worked up the courage and meekly corrected myself, "Yes, Roberta?"

"I understand from Finney that you're 'on the loose.' I want to meet with you. Let's have tea tomorrow, at teatime, 4 o'clock."

"Yes, Ms. Fla—Roberta."

Roberta chortled. I made Roberta laugh, *the* Roberta—because no one on this planet had ever graced that name like she had. I jotted down instructions on how to get to her place and hastily hung up the phone.

I didn't sleep that night because I didn't know what I would say. I had told myself that I would do anything to make it. What did that mean? What could I do? Myriad thoughts were racing through my mind. This whole predicament was so surreal that all I could do was chuckle nervously, as I tried to will myself to sleep.

The next morning was a glorious day. Central Park was alight with fall colors. Reflections from the skyscrapers cast dancing prisms on the paths and dew tipped the grass like Swarovski crystals on the ears of passing women. The walk from my apartment on West 55th street was not a long one at all, but I always wanted to leave plenty of time to arrive anywhere to protect my mind from feeling hurried. Since I was an hour early, I decided to sit on a bench near the site that would one day become Strawberry Fields. I ran simulations of the interview in my head. What could she possibly ask? I told myself they were just words, thoughts in the air. My job was to catch a strand and make it my own. It was soon time to cross the street. I entered the Dakota, Ms. Flack's building, and went to the reception so they could inform her of my arrival. One of the doormen asked me to wait for a second and then politely pointed, "Miss Bridges, you can take that elevator."

At this moment, everything was becoming so real. I entered the elevator and sat on a little bulkhead, big enough for just two people. Noticing the shallowness of my breath, I inhaled sharply, held it for five seconds and then released it—trying not to think. Fortunately, the words that insisted on entering my mind were consoling and cajoling, "You've done it. You're here. You've received this gift."

The elevator stopped a few floors up and a person entered and sat next to me while offering a humble "Good day," in a soothing British accent. The elevator started to move. It was a very slow elevator, one of the slowest I had ever been on. As I sat there, I could feel a palpable energy next to me. In my nervousness, I hadn't looked up when the man had greeted me, simply responding with a quiet "Good afternoon," as my eyes drilled holes into the pristine, tiled floor. But his energy was overwhelming and so I slowly turned my gaze to my seatmate. Upon meeting his eyes, I had to do everything in my power not to gasp. John Lennon was sitting right next to me, exuding an air of genuine humanity and decency that continues to touch me every time I think about it. We rode that slow-moving elevator in silence, but that moment reverberates loudly in my memory until this day. We reached the 7th floor. I exited first and intuitively turned to the left. He went to the right and upon stopping at his door, he repeated, "Good day." This time I managed to enunciate, "You, too," with a little more conviction.

After I rang Ms. Flack's bell, her housekeeper opened the door. I stepped inside and as soon as she closed the door, I leaned against it and slid down to the floor. She started screaming "Ms. Flack, Ms. Flack! There's something wrong!" I just sat there as Roberta came running down the hall. There I was, slumped over with Roberta Flack—*the* Roberta Flack—hovering over me, asking, "What's wrong, what's wrong?"

I somehow muttered "Ms. Flack. Roberta, I can't have the meeting today. I can't think."

"What happened?"

"John Lennon was on the elevator with me."

Roberta started laughing hysterically. After a moment, she calmed down enough to say, "Let me make some tea," then she helped me to my feet. As we were having tea, she giggled, "Child, I see him in his boxer shorts all the time because he never bothers to put on clothes when taking out the garbage!" The image of John Lennon carrying garbage in his boxers helped counteract my initial shock and I began to feel more like myself.

I appreciated her trying to make light of the situation, but I still asked if I could go home. Both she and the housekeeper were laughing as they walked me to the door. I wanted to tell them that it wasn't because I was star-struck. It was because this man had changed the world. But I didn't think they would believe me, so I thanked them for their time and took the stairs—not the elevator—down to the ground floor. I crossed the street and returned to where I had been sitting in the park. I looked long and hard at the Dakota before making my way home.

My less-than-professional performance that day had not deterred Roberta, surprisingly. She called with a list of five people who she wanted me to meet while she was away on tour behind the Iron Curtain. "Her people," she called them. She gave me the name of the president of her record company, Ahmet Ertegun and his right-hand woman, Noreen Woods; her agent, Marty Klein at the William Morris Agency; Michael Zink, who was in charge of her equipment and staging; and Joe Ferla, her engineer. She was giving me her key people. I knew zero about the music industry.

The following day, I went to meet Marty Klein at 1350 6th Avenue. Roberta had told him that she was interested in having me join the team. She had given him some information about me—my experience as a model, my studies at FIT and how I was interested in a career change. I dressed as nicely as I could and also mentally dressed up my confidence before going to see him.

Marty was exceedingly abrupt with me from the moment we met. "What do you think you can do? How do you feel you can be of assistance to Roberta? You are nobody," he intoned with overwhelming haughtiness.

Not one to BS, I told him I had no idea. "I'm just here because she asked me to come and meet with you. I'm sure she'll tell me."

He sat back for a while and then leaned forward and said, "Young lady, you'll be crawling on your knees back to 7th Avenue." And just as curtly, the meeting was over. I remember walking home and asking myself defiantly, "Why would he say that? What did it matter that my background was in fashion if I was willing to do whatever necessary to assist Roberta?" I swallowed his potshot on the fashion industry, encapsulated by the iconic 7th Avenue, like a bitter pill. I never forgot

that moment. While I decided not to hold anything against him personally—grudges have a habit of destroying the one with the grudge long
before they can do damage to the recipient—I vowed that I would never
be crawling anywhere, ever. All I could do now was wait until Roberta
returned from her tour. As the holidays approached, I thought about
contacting her, but then decided to give her space and follow up in the
New Year. Two days after she returned to New York, she called me and
offered me the job. Marty Klein would have to watch someone else crawl
back to 7th Avenue.

Early in 1980, I went on the road with Roberta. She was touring the
country and I was responsible for dealing with the media. I made sure
that they did what they were supposed to do, because if they didn't, I
would confiscate their cameras. I also supported the musicians and got
them what they needed. I loved watching Roberta perform every day to
thousands and thousands of people. She made them so happy just by
sharing her gifts with them. I really felt a sense of purpose being a part of
that, but it wasn't an easy job.

Of all the places I've been in my years in the music industry, our
one-month stint in Vegas was by far the most depressing. Bad food,
gaudy decorations, nothing to do but what you shouldn't be doing. I
remember feeling like I was suffocating in my hotel room. Once, I called
maintenance to ask them to open my window. The man on the line said
outright, "Miss, we don't open the windows because people commit
suicide." I was also amazed how there were no clocks and no natural light

when we were indoors. I felt my soul slowly hibernating from the lack of sun since we were working all the time and couldn't make it outside often. To make matters worse, I was exhausted from constantly having to stand up to the band and remind them that they had instructed me not to give them their per diems (their daily allowances) while in Vegas. In fact, I even had each sign a paper stipulating this. They knew themselves and had been worried about gambling all their pay away. It was not until we left Vegas, that they thanked me for keeping them to their word and apologized for any insults they had hurled my way during momentary (and regular) bouts of anger.

However, it was the position that Marty put me in with the promoters that really soured the experience for me. Marty called me two nights before we were supposed to leave Vegas to tell me that all the money owed to us had yet to arrive in New York. We were talking about $100,000, which would probably be worth four times that in today's dollars. Instead of handling it on his end, like he should have, Marty told me to collect the rest of the money. This was not in my job description. The contract specifically stated that if the full amount was not with the agent, Roberta would not get on stage. The heat was on me. If I had told Roberta, there would have been chaos. You didn't mess with her, because she was fierce and would have no problem with cancelling a concert. I told my counterpart Michael Zink—an Irish guy from the south side of Chicago—about what was happening and he agreed that Roberta had to do the show. We couldn't imagine the fallout if she failed to perform at the culminating performance of a sold-out run.

As soon as it was all over, the band couldn't get out of there fast enough. Everyone had loaded into the van except for Mike and me. We nervously lingered behind to figure out how to get the money that the promoters owed us. When Roberta realized that Mike and I were missing, she came out and found us. I convinced her that I needed to stay back with Mike and make sure that all the equipment was packed up correctly. A month in one place was a long time, so we wanted to confirm that everything was as it should have been. Once she left, Mike and I looked at each other and he said, "I'm moving your room next to mine and don't leave your room without me." Once I switched rooms, I called the promoters, who were two brothers and told them that we were not leaving until they brought us the balance due. I then called Marty and told him that Roberta was on her way, but that Mike and I were going to stay until this whole mess was straightened out.

The brothers did not sound happy with me while I was on the phone, but I reiterated that I was not leaving my room until they brought me the money. There was silence on the other line and then a click. Mike and I had adjoining rooms at this point and we paced between them as we waited to see if they would make good on what they owed. We then rattled off different scenarios of what they would do to us if they decided not to pay. All scenarios ended up with us dead and buried somewhere in the desert. Several hours later, there was a rough knock on my door and a burly guy with a painstakingly groomed moustache, barged in when I opened it. He dropped a suitcase on the bed and asked in a huff if I needed to count the money in front of him. I responded with a curt, "Yes." Then, Mike and I started tallying up the bills. Normally, promoters don't pay in cash, especially when the fee is this high. This all would've been much simpler if the money had been wired to Marty's office like it was supposed to have been. Once I verified that it was indeed all there, I thanked the burly man with a forced smile and escorted him out the room. Mike and I grabbed our things and practically ran out the door. Once we were on our plane, Mike turned to me and laughed, "You are one crazy bitch. There was a place in the middle of the desert with our names on it."

I simply replied, "But we're not buried in the desert, Mike. We're here. Still alive."

For my next birthday, Mike gave me a pair of ruby slippers. When I opened the package he grinned and said, "You're not in Kansas anymore." It was one of the most thoughtful gifts I had ever received. Meanwhile, when I think about how badly that whole incident could've gone, I tell myself that Marty Klein was the one that should have crawled on his knees to 7th Avenue.

The Vegas incident gave me confidence that I could do this job, but it also made me realize how volatile this business could be and impressed upon me that I needed to learn the ropes quickly. Fortunately, I never experienced anything like that sticky situation in Vegas for the rest of my time with Roberta, since the promoters that we interacted with were usually very professional. As such, I picked up the trade through normal run-of-the-mill job experience even though my responsibilities were quite varied.

In May, we headed to Ecuador for the first of several concerts throughout Latin America. Leading up to our trip, I was in charge of making sure that the crew had all their travel documents in order. Roberta informed me a few weeks before we began the tour that she was going to take a male backup singer along. He had been successful as the voice of Coca

Cola, singing jingles in their ads, but he admired Roberta so much that he gave up that relatively lucrative career to be Roberta's backup singer. From my first interaction with him, I was taken aback by how sweet and sensitive he was. That was the moment when I became one of Luther Vandross's biggest fans.

We were all set to fly to Guayaquil, Ecuador, when I informed Luther that he would be sitting next to me on the plane. Roberta had thought that would be best because he didn't know anyone and could be shy when first meeting people. Roberta was always very concerned about the treatment of her band, backup singers and crew. He seemed relieved when I told him of the seating arrangements and he confided that he had a fear of flying. He asked if I could remind him to take his medication, which would help him get through the flight. He was indeed nervous the whole time we were in the air and while I tended not to interact too heavily with my colleagues when on the road—just enough to be effective at my job—I realized that he needed small talk to help keep his mind off of the fact that we were several thousand feet in the air. He relaxed once we landed and got a little better each time we flew from country to country across South America.

During his stint with Roberta, he was the only person I let book a room on the same floor as me, other than James Finney, of course. Everyone knew that my room was off limits and I would usually not divulge where I was staying to anyone other than Roberta. However, I saw Luther as a brother. He filled some sort of gap that was formed when I left my brother Robert all those years ago and that reopened once again with Jimi Hendrix's gut-wrenching death. Luther seemed to appreciate the special treatment that I gave him. By rooming near him, I could be a more effective friend. Luther was always on a diet and needed some outside influence to keep him on track. I accepted the task of keeping him from ordering room service. If I heard the knock of a hotel attendant bringing up a plate to his room, I would intercept the delivery and send it back to the kitchen. Luther relied on me to provide him the willpower that he sometimes lacked.

One night, after a show near the end of our tour of the Americas, Roberta asked me to bring Luther into her dressing room. Other than Finney, he was pretty much the only man she ever allowed back there. Luther was quite at home among women and was often the only male backup singer. I went off to handle some post-show business and when I returned, I saw Luther leave Roberta's room crying. Tears streaked the foundation and powder they put on all the performers, regardless of gender, to cut down on glare. I held him in a long embrace until his sobs had somewhat subsided. Then I asked him if he wanted to tell me what happened. He finally managed to explain that Roberta had fired him. I was in disbelief. Here was a man who had the silkiest voice that you could imagine. He was a joy to work with and a consummate gentleman. I could not think of a better person for Roberta to have by her side. After I walked him to some of the other singers so they could provide moral support, I knocked on Roberta's dressing room door.

"Roberta, why did you fire Luther?" I asked after she let me in.

"He's too good," she replied. I thought to myself that Roberta had one of the best voices in the business. There's no way that she would be threatened by Luther. Perhaps reading my mind, she continued, "He needs to go out on his own. He can't be hiding in my shadow. I know people like that. They are content blending into the background for their whole careers. And I don't blame them. It takes a certain type of personality and ego to be front and center night after night, promoting yourself and reminding those in the industry that pull the strings that you're more than just a pretty face and a soulful voice. Perhaps Luther is too sweet for that life, but I would be doing the whole world a disservice if I didn't at least force him to wrestle with the possibility of stardom."

I didn't see Luther very much after our tour ended. He took Roberta's advice and launched a solo career. He did well on the R&B scene throughout the eighties, but really left his mark on the larger music scene in the nineties. His success always made my heart explode with joy. His stroke in 2003 and untimely death a couple of years later, took him away from us too soon. Even though I believe that they would have continued to be wonderful together, I'm so grateful that Roberta was intuitive enough to let him go so that he could better share his gift with the world.[3]

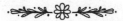

In early December of 1980, we embarked on our Down Under tour after a short hiatus. We had been basking in the success of our Latin America tour since our return to the US, but now had to get back to work. Playing in front of sold-out crowds in places such as Ecuador, Chile, and Venezuela, we had been heartened to see Roberta enjoying as much love from Spanish-speaking countries as she did from her native United States. It was around then that I became fully aware of how transcendent her music was. I already understood how impressive it was that her soulful stylings spoke to mainstream society by crossing racial

---

3. For more information about Luther Vandross, see Seymour's *Luther*.

lines, as well as those drawn by tastes in genre. For instance, she was the first African American woman to have multiple number one pop hits as a solo artist. However, it was the Latin America tour that brought home how powerful a Black woman's music could be on the global stage.

I had now been on the road with Roberta for about a year and had settled into my role as tour manager. It pretty much meant that I was in charge of keeping people on time, in good condition, and true to their word. Howard King, Roberta's drummer—probably one of the most talented in the business—would jokingly call me persnickety. He knew that my word was my bond. There was no ambiguity in what I said and I took no excuses. Being on the road with a bunch of guys could be difficult, so I made sure to set the tone from the start. Howard only crossed me a couple times before he realized that I meant business and he became very good at following all my instructions. Reggie Lucas and James Mtume took a little more work, but in the end, we behaved like a well-oiled machine. I figured that I was doing something right when, one day, Howard asked how long I had been in the business. He didn't believe me when I told him that working with Roberta was my first gig.

Through these relationships that I cultivated on the road, I became proficient in communication. The band would do what I said out of respect for me, because they knew that I respected them as well. I also had to devise strategies to work with the people that I only encountered sporadically and therefore with whom I lacked time to build rapport. Sometimes, I was able to get my point across diplomatically. Other times, I had to be a real hard ass. The scary situation in Vegas was an example of the latter. Making sure that the promoter in Australia provided Roberta with Courvoisier VSOP cognac at every concert was an instance of the former.

The rider of Roberta's contract expressly stated that she would always receive a bottle of Courvoisier VSOP backstage. She was known for not being a big drinker. In fact, she would usually just have a cup of tea, which I was in charge of bringing her, before any concert. However, I understood the rider to be the word of God. Whatever was in there, I made sure she got. For our first concert in Australia, the promoter stopped by and asked if everything was okay. "Everything is very comfortable, but there is just one thing: this isn't Courvoisier VSOP," I told him while holding up the bottle of brandy for his inspection.

He laughed awkwardly, not sure if I was joking or not, before replying, "It's not Courvoisier VSOP, Alvenia. But it's one of the finest brandies in Australia."

"That may be the case, but it's not Courvoisier VSOP."

"You can't be serious."

I just flashed him my biggest smile. I had decided a long time ago that the best way to get something was to kill people with kindness. There was no malice in my eyes or a desire to humiliate him, just a conviction that I needed to do whatever the contract said had to be done. After his complaining about having to send someone out to the liquor store and my meeting his protests with that steadfast smile, he relented. I never had to tell him about the Courvoisier again.

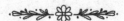

My ability to give people who I cared about the things that they wanted was a power I was grateful to have, especially when my actions could mitigate some of the worst aspects of society. Nothing illustrated this more than when I stood up to racism and other types of discrimination. For instance, while waiting in line at Immigration at Sydney Airport with the rest of the crew, I noticed Finney, who was a few people in front of me in line, suddenly tense up as he was answering the immigration officer's questions. Finney was the type of person that could never go unnoticed. That day, he was wearing a white kaftan, that seemed to be embroidered with the long braids that spiraled down his back. He was visibly shaken, so I approached them and overheard the officer asking questions that seemed irrelevant to the task at hand. I then looked at the other booths and realized that practically all of Roberta's entourage—band members who stood out mainly because they were Black with dreadlocks—were in the same predicament. I asked the Atlantic Records representative, who had met us at the airport, to go to each person in our group and offer assistance. I was hoping that his whiteness and his status with Atlantic Records could counter the obvious systemic profiling that was happening there. I then turned to the officer harassing Finney and said with as little emotion as possible, "Roberta Flack is performing one month of sold-out shows. If you don't let this gentleman in, I will make sure that this whole tour gets cancelled." The officer glared at me in much the same way as the police officer who pinned me against the ground all those years ago in Kansas. But I was a different person, embodying a different character in the same tired story of racism and I was hell-bent on coming out unscathed this time. The officer relented and after he spoke with the other officers, all of Roberta's crew was able to set foot on Australian soil.

At the heart of it, Finney was a delicate soul. He didn't understand why people treated him the way that they did sometimes, whether it be for his race or his sexuality. In that moment, it was my task to protect

Finney from any bigotry directed at him. Seething from the realization that Australia was no different from the United States in how it treated people of color, I learned that being Black was a constant struggle globally. I was becoming an expert at ignoring the insidious hum of racism long enough to handle whatever business I needed to tend to.

While my time in Australia taught me that America did not have a monopoly on racism, I also learned the importance of transnational solidarity among peoples of color. Each day while in Sydney, I went to a lush, public park next to the hotel in order to have some space by myself in nature. One day, upon returning to the hotel, I saw an Indigenous Australian man at the base of the escalator leading up to the lobby. He was dressed in a crisp shirt and dress slacks and held a long, shiny, meticulously painted, wooden object. A security guard glared at him from the lobby doors. There had been an exchange between them, judging from the tension that buzzed in the air.

Based on my experience at the airport, as well as the fact that people of color stood out in places like this hotel, I made my way over to the man and asked if there was anything that I could help him with. He smiled and lifted the beautiful carving in his hands. I had never seen a didgeridoo before. He explained how his tribe wanted to give Roberta this present as a show of respect and since he had seen me with her earlier, he asked if I would give it to her. When the security guards would not let him into the hotel to leave it at the front desk, he had decided to wait for me in hopes that I would be sympathetic. I told him, no, I would not take it up to her. He would have to do so himself. I then asked him to accompany me into the hotel.

As we reached the door, the guard snarled at the man about how he had already told him that he wasn't allowed to enter. I countered that this man was my guest and would indeed be entering with me. I then called for the manager and explained that if this hotel was going to discriminate against Aboriginal people, we were going to find a different place to stay. The manager finally yielded and let us both pass. I led him up to Roberta's room. As I watched Roberta accept the gift that this man presented on behalf of his tribe with utmost joy, I decided not to get angry that this moment almost didn't happen because of some ignorant security guards and unstated hotel policies. Instead, I wanted to focus on the resilience and patience that paved the way for him to share that special moment with someone as deserving as Roberta.

Other than the few racist incidents that Roberta never found out about, our time in Australia was going well, as the fans' energy left everyone riding high. On December ninth, a little after a week of being in Australia, we headed to New Zealand for a short break. The four-hour flight seemed short compared to our flight from Los Angeles to Sydney. The weather was sunny, as summer was in full swing in the southern hemisphere. As we landed in Auckland, we prepared ourselves for the onslaught of media attention as soon as we deplaned. In those days, reporters would meet you at the airport, so you had to be stunning even before you left the plane. Roberta was in the back of the plane with Finney, getting her hair and makeup done. The crew disembarked first to meet with an Atlantic Record representative. As soon as I exited the plane, the representative gently pulled me to the side, looked me squarely in the eyes without trying to conceal his devastation and slowly recounted how, while we were in the air, John Lennon had been shot and killed outside the Dakota. Before I could register my own emotions, he suggested that I should be the one to tell Roberta. He knew how fond Roberta and John had been of each other. It should come from someone close to Roberta, not from a TV screen.

"What about the press? Won't they bring it up when speaking to Roberta?" I inquired.

"They've been told to not mention it out of respect for her. The whole world is in shock. They can't even articulate their feelings, let alone report on it. It's up to you to carry on, get everyone to the hotel and check in. The driver won't say anything."

The ride to the hotel seemed like an eternity. I was struggling under the weight of this secret—a secret that the whole world shared with me, but that I couldn't tell until the right moment. The band and Roberta were oblivious. It felt almost like a betrayal, but I wanted to do it in private.

As soon as I checked in, I went directly to her room. She greeted me with a smile, always cloaked in a magnetic energy and infectious happiness, even after flying. As her fire-lit eyes met mine, the seriousness on my face quickly extinguished her joy. I didn't know what to say and I met her new look of concern with silence.

"Is my mother okay?" she pleaded. Her mother had been unwell. I moved toward her, but, instinctively, she backed up while demanding that I tell her what the matter was. I started to move furniture in case, well, I don't know why. I guess in case she fainted. Besides, my fingers just wanted to fidget while I searched for the words. At last, I couldn't stall any longer and I told her that John Lennon was dead.

She screamed and dropped to the floor, rolling back and forth. There was so much emotion and pain. She was on her stomach. Face buried into the rug. Wails muffled by plush fibers. After pounding the floor with her fists and then convulsing into sobs, she remained there. After a moment, I thought that she had cried herself to sleep. But slowly, she picked herself up off the floor, eyes bloodshot and salty tears streaking her face. She turned to me and said in a tone of upmost seriousness, "Get the band together. Get the promoter."

Without a word, I left her room and gathered the band.

"What's going on?" One of the members complained. "We have three days off. I want to explore New Zealand." They didn't know what had happened. They hadn't turned on the TV.

I simply told them that Roberta wanted to see them. We all went to her suite. As she broke the news to them, their indignation turned to shock and then heartache. Working through our swirling emotions, we brainstormed how we could best memorialize John Lennon. Instead of a three-day rest break, we told the promoter to get a studio for us so that we could rehearse something special for our concerts once we returned to Sydney. Our bodies were there, but our minds weren't. We couldn't stop thinking about how this wonderful man was stripped from our lives so suddenly.

The first concert back in Australia was overwhelmingly amazing. We were on a mission to express how we felt about what happened to John Lennon. For us to be able to share that with the audience was an emotional rollercoaster. The whole audience held candles at each and every performance. There were no words, but a feeling. Every year on Roberta's birthday, I think about sitting next to him in that elevator and about Roberta trying to calm me down with the image of him taking out the trash in his boxer shorts. His presence exuded so much light and energy. His gift to the world tells it all. He was a messenger, just like Jimi.

Fig. 12. Alvenia reminiscing about the time the Rolling Stones and other musicians met Princess Di. Original by unknown. By Maya Angela Smith.

*Fig. 13. Alvenia at Rolling Stones concert in Torino. Original
by unknown. By Maya Angela Smith.*

The photo of members of the Rolling Stones and other celebrities meeting Princess Di (Fig. 12) is one of Alvenia's most cherished memories. As
Princess Di smiles and greets each musician standing in a line, Alvenia is
off to the side, behind the scenes, yet holding her own in a dress by Haitian
fashion designer Fabrice Simon. Alvenia was instrumental in getting this
meeting to happen. For Buckingham Palace to send Alvenia a photo of
the moment, along with a quick note, meant everything to her, because it
acknowledged a recognition of her abilities.

When Alvenia looks at a photo of herself (Fig. 13) in an unauthorized Italian publication of the Rolling Stones on tour in Torino, she can't help but laugh. She says that her expression captured her mood the whole time she was there as Mick Jagger's personal business liaison. It was hot. It was chaotic. And her Italian counterparts were always trying to sneak things by her. She perfected the "don't mess with me" stare during those few days being on the road in Italy. However, she reflects lovingly on her experience there as well, because it was at that moment that she really began to shine in her new career. She found her groove and her voice and became a formidable part of the crew.

Roberta Flack took a chance on me when there was really no reason to. There were people like Marty Klein who expected my failure. What was a fashion model with no music experience going to bring to the high-stress, fast-paced life of the music industry? Besides, Roberta was known as the toughest woman in music. She was a serious businesswoman and a musical perfectionist, who expected the most out of everybody, especially herself. But high expectations were my fuel source. I relished challenges and got shit done. While I had never had any formal training until that point, I ended up getting my PhD in showbusiness from Roberta Flack. Roberta taught me everything I knew, so when Mick Jagger approached me in early 1981 to become his personal business liaison, I knew that I was up to the task.

"I've heard you're one of the baddest in the business, Alvenia. I could really use someone like you on the road," Mick told me over the phone when trying to make the case for working with him. It gave me immense pride to see that others were taking notice of my abilities. More importantly, Roberta gave me her blessings, seemingly content that her protégé was spreading her wings. Just like with Luther Vandross, she knew when it was time to push us out of the nest.

After I accepted Mick's offer, he sent me to an office just across the street from Carnegie Hall to meet with his promoter, Bill Graham, before we hit the road. I didn't know him and after our first meeting, I wasn't sure if I wanted to know him. When I arrived, I walked into pandemonium, which I soon learned was the normal setting. There was a giant mirror that Bill used as a whiteboard. With each sleeve pulled up by a garter belt, he wrote, "JFK, sold out. 8 minutes." After this, the whole production crew was talking to Bill at once and I just stood there looking dumbfounded. He turned around and said to me, "What the fuck do you think you can do for this tour, young woman?" Then he turned back around. While I was appreciative that he addressed me as "young woman" instead of "girl" or "girlie" (or worse), I was still having flashbacks to Marty Klein. No one seemed to take me seriously. "Whatever you say, sir." I then glanced over to Jan Simmons, Bill's assistant and the left and right side of his brain, who gave me the "don't leave" look.

Bill turned once more and left me with the following advice, "If you ever need anything and you don't tell me, you're out. I'll see you in Philly."

After I exited the building, I leaned against the façade and thought to myself, *Why did he speak to me that way?* But I couldn't dwell on it too much. I had work to do.

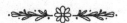

I officially started as Mick's personal business liaison in mid-September of 1981. Basically, if anyone needed to talk to Mick, they would have to go through me. I set his schedule and made sure that he knew about everything from important events to mundane activities.

Right before we went on tour, he called out of the blue, "I'm sorry to call so late, Alvenia, but would you mind going out with me tonight? I wanted to check someone out." He was always very polite, but not someone to hang out with employees outside of work, so I was surprised by his invitation.

He summoned a car and met me at the front of my apartment building. He then proceeded to spend the whole ride trying to make me laugh at his jokes. He always did this because he knew that I never laughed at or understood anyone's jokes. As usual, he failed, though I appreciated the effort. My brain seemed to be wired differently than everyone else and nothing made this more evident than humor. We soon arrived at a funky club on the Lower East Side called CBGBs—a place that was real cool, real New York and full of people of all races and nationalities. As we made our way backstage, a petite man with striking eyeliner, garter belts, and stockings strutted across the stage almost like a contortionist. He had this amazing range, impressing me with how his voice could travel seemingly into the stratosphere. As I listened to the performer belt those high notes, Mick told me he would be right back.

Mick was the one who always found the opening acts for their tours and really liked to push the envelope with the groups he showcased. I thought to myself, *I don't know if the world has seen anyone like the lead singer*. On the ride back home, Mick asked for my opinion. I couldn't really articulate what I was thinking, so I just said, "It was wild." Not another word was spoken about it. It was not until I saw him perform again, this time at Memorial Coliseum in Los Angeles a few weeks later, that I was reunited with this mystery man.

As an opening act for the Stones, that enigma of a person, supported by his band, started doing his thing and all of a sudden, 100,000 people went berserk and not in a good way. By the third song, the audience was throwing things at him and cursing him violently. Bill Graham grabbed the mic and called for security. The singer, who I really thought was ahead of his time, ran off stage, jumped in his car and drove off. There was sheer and utter chaos while Mick tried to figure out what was going on. As things settled down, Mick told me to go find our disgraced performer, but he seemed to have vanished without a trace. I found out later that he had retreated back to his native Minnesota. However, I had a suspicion that this would not be the last we heard of Prince. Proving my intuition right, he came back with a vengeance—defying the odds for decades. Very few would reach the heights that Prince did. When I learned of his passing, I couldn't stop thinking about how the world was robbed of another musical genius. Fortunately for us, Prince continues to change the world with the music he left us.

By the third month as Mick's personal business liaison, I had things down. I was in my groove and feeling great, even though most of the time I was flying by the seat of my pants. We kept a hectic schedule but had the day off for Thanksgiving, which we spent in Syracuse, New York. Early that morning, I went to the newsstand to get papers for about twenty people. As I was returning on the moving sidewalk with the bundle of papers in my arms, I saw Bill coming toward me on the opposite moving side.

"Good morning," I said as I passed him.

He replied, "Good morning."

It was like any other morning exchange we had had. However, after I stepped of the conveyor, I saw him in my periphery disembarking his sidewalk and then hopping back on the other side to move in my direction. Expecting that he was going to berate me for some mistake he had just remembered, I turned to face him and readied my stance.

Instead, he said, "You're fuckin' bad."

I dropped the papers. There was no better compliment than being labeled the good type of bad. For Bill to show his appreciation for my work was like winning an Oscar. He was not known for being generous with his praise. He then gave me a huge hug.

Bill cursed at everyone all the time. I had encountered it the first time we met, when I was convinced that he thought hiring me was a bad idea. For him to use his favorite expletive in a positive sense was the highest commendation and I have treasured that moment for the rest of my life. From then on, our mutual respect became more and more pronounced. People often confused our admiration for lust and whispered about how we were an item. It was their fantasy. Our relationship was strictly professional. But there is no denying, I did—and still do—love him dearly.

After Thanksgiving, the Stones had about three more weeks on tour. Because I was constantly living "in the now," I was blindsided when I realized that Kansas City was our penultimate stop. Kemper Arena, while technically in Missouri, sits on the Kansas-Missouri border, less than five miles from my childhood home. For the guys on the road, this was nothing more than any other performance venue, unremarkable because the road makes all destinations blend into indistinction.

I hadn't thought much about Kansas since my escape. I had a job to do and tried to focus all my energy on the Stones, but in the back of my mind, I knew that I would have to make peace with the city of my childhood. For almost twenty years, I had made good on my promise to never return. Was I really ready to break that promise?

We were performing for two nights and after a brief moment in which two warring factions of my mind debated the issue, I felt compelled to cross over into Kansas and stop by various locations in my hometown during my free time. I passed through parts of town I wasn't allowed to enter when I was young. "Whites only" signs had steered me clear of the places I wanted to be. Any time I thought about being defiant, the storeowners' stares would quickly put me back in my place. It had always been difficult to pass by store fronts parading their best wares. Zonnetta had a taste for fancy things. She was a beautiful woman with impeccable taste. When she saw something that she wanted, she would put it on layaway and then work really hard until she earned enough money to buy it for herself. I was always so impressed with her work ethic and wanted to emulate her, so I would save my pocket money from mowing lawns and shoveling snow, in order to purchase little presents for her that I knew she had put on layaway. This was before I gave up on the dream of buying her love. Having that realization sooner would've saved me a lot of heartbreak because it was always the white stores—the stores that refused to serve me—that had the most coveted items.

Those signs had long been taken down, but as I walked into both the haunts of my youth and the forbidden places that no longer barred my entrance, I became overwhelmed by numbness. There was absolutely no feeling or emotion in me. I thought to myself in a surprisingly clinical way, "I have conquered." This place had made me not like America, but its depravity had also led to my emancipation. One thing was for certain during my childhood: if I stayed, I would wind up dead or in jail; therefore, I was forced to think larger. Through that need to dream big, I figured out how to see the world instead. I firmly believed that I was not put on this planet to be unhappy, thus I resolved to make sure my beautiful skin never kept me from happiness. My return to Kansas with the Stones was a testament to that.

In early 1982, we had a few months between the American and the European tours to recuperate and prepare. Mick had a daily exercise regimen, wherein he ran at least five miles followed by weights and high intensity training with his personal trainer. His approach to his health bordered on religious, but also allowed him to run across the stage for two and a half hours non-stop. His being one of the greatest showmen to ever grace the stage didn't keep him from constantly trying to improve.

One morning, he called me up to see if I could find him a dance teacher. I set him up with a friend of a friend, an Irish woman with flaming red hair. When she arrived at his place near 81st and Amsterdam, he led her to the library, because the wood floor was smooth and there was room to put up a portable mirror. After a quick warm up, she gave him some basic steps, but he just couldn't get the hang of it. After an hour of fumbling around, she told him straight, "Look, hon, your feet just can't feel the rhythm. Why don't you just keep doing what you're doing?" We all had a laugh and from that moment on, Mick fully embraced his stage-strutting ways. It had worked for him all those years, so why try to be something he wasn't?

Being back in New York City also meant that I started crossing paths with Jerry again. It was difficult being both Jerry's friend and Mick's right-hand woman. They both had so many secrets to keep and as it stated in my contract, I don't deal with anyone's personal business. I felt like I had this weird split loyalty, no matter how much I tried to keep my eyes shut, I would learn things that frustrated me. It was well known that Mick was a philanderer, but because I refused to have any more contact than necessary, he never flaunted this character trait in front of me. Jerry, however, was unconcerned with keeping her improprieties from me. Years earlier, before I even felt any sort of allegiance to Mick, I had to watch her cozy up to him, even though she was in a relationship with Brian Ferry. In all fairness, Mick had still been married to Bianca Jagger, so they both were cheating on their partners, but I never had to lie to Bianca like Jerry had forced me to lie to Brian. I hated lying and had begun to resent her for the predicaments that she always put me in. At one point, I had become so tired of fielding Brian's increasingly frantic phone calls that I marched down to Mick's place and dragged her back to our apartment. I then told her to handle her shit because I was tired of doing it for her.

Considering how I had explained to her why the whole Brian situation made me upset, I figured she would spare me from any of her other indiscretions, but she ignored my pleas. One time after she and Mick became serious, she tricked me into going to Spain for a vacation. I should've learned after Texas, that when Jerry wants to take you on a trip, you are getting more than you bargained for. As we sat there relaxing in first class, she confided in me how happy she was because she was going to rendezvous with her current lover and my travelling with her provided cover. I wanted to hurt her physically, but summoned every ounce of civility in me so that I wouldn't act on this impulse. I asked the flight attendant if I could be moved to the economy section. The attendant first thought I was joking, but as soon as she saw the flames in my eyes, she arranged for me to have a new seat right away. The poor woman genuinely looked upset and concerned; I must have had murder written all over my face. Perhaps Jerry was playing Mick's game as well as he played it, but I wanted no part of either's games.

One of the biggest betrayals, however, was in 1984 when Jerry honored me by asking me to be godmother to her first child, Elizabeth, and then took it back. By this time, her and Mick's relationship had spanned twenty years. I had been there for Jerry as she threw herself into impending motherhood. I was there for her when she wasn't initially able to conceive. She tried to do everything to get pregnant and even entertained old wives' tales such as eating more sausages. Once she got pregnant, I became an even greater presence in her life, throwing her a baby shower and helping her keep doctor's appointments. We were finally rekindling the close bond we had had all those years ago—I couldn't believe a decade had passed—when we were bold, brash, young women. We talked about all the things we would do together as her family grew. While there had been numerous events in our friendship that had whittled away my trust in her, those fractures were finally on the mend. So, when she turned to me one evening and told me that I was no longer going to be the godmother, I was more hurt than I expected.

She reasoned, "It's not me. Mick doesn't want you to be the godmother. We have chosen Charlie Watts' wife Shirley instead."

I had no idea if that was really the case. Perhaps she didn't have much of a say in the matter. It shouldn't have been a big deal, but it was the sort of flippant way that she told me that really cut deep.

Our always tenuous friendship continued to dissolve over the years. It wasn't one thing but a series of scrapes and bruises that I was tired of bandaging. We finally grew apart for good and haven't been in touch since. Our mutual friend, Geraldine, tries periodically to open channels between us and perhaps one day it will happen. But old wounds can take an eternity to heal.

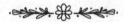

While a lifetime of hurt and betrayal from those I yearned to call friends or family made me wary of any type of deep relationship, my career was the one thing that didn't disappoint, because I had more control and could dictate things on my terms. The Stones headed to Europe in late spring of 1982 to continue promoting the *Tattoo You* album. It was the highest of highs to be a part of such a production. Every concert, Bill would introduce the show, "Ladies and Gentlemen, thank you for waiting ..." and no matter where I was, I would scream "Yes!" Could you believe I got *paid* to do this? It was so special for me to see how happy people became when the Stones got on stage. Often, the audience seemed to view these concerts as family-friendly experiences. People would carry babies on their shoulders and the crowd always represented a range of ages. There was intergenerational appeal. One of the most memorable scenes was at the Waldbühne, in what was then West Berlin, when the Stones released thousands of red balloons into the air in June of 1982.

That moment even inspired audience member Carlos Karges to write the instant hit "99 Luftballons" for the band Nena.[1] The peacefulness of that experience contrasted heavily with the Stones 1965 concert there, when the Waldbühne had been practically destroyed after fans had stormed the stage and clashed with police armed with fire hoses and billy clubs.

The infamous '65 concert was a reminder that there was always a chance for mayhem. People were often drunk, stoned, or both. The long waits after the opening acts did not help the situation, so people would get unruly until the Stones finally came on. However, there were seldom any serious issues in the years I was involved, which was even more surprising considering how large the crowds were. The Stones' security was partially to thank for this. They only hired ex-Green Berets, led by the imposing Jim Callaghan, who had his work cut out for him, since his primary duty was to keep Keith Richards safe from himself.

Watching the ex-Green Berets in action was a thing of beauty. Even though they were all muscle, they had charming ways of disarming people. Twice, I saw Jim put his arm around somebody and say, "I really don't think you're going to do what I think is on your mind." That was all it took. The concert in Torino in mid-July '82 was the most challenging because everyone—the crowd, management—seemed to want to break all our rules. It didn't help that it was the dead of summer and people were practically dying of heat stroke. Forty-five minutes or so before our first show at the Stadio Comunale, I heard on my walkie talkie "loose cannon, loose cannon," which was our code for someone taking unauthorized photos. When we found the perpetrators, I instructed my

---

1. See Patton's "Ballons."

guys to grab the cameras and take out the film. They then gave me all the cameras so that I could put them in the trailer backstage until after the show. We always compensated these fans for their destroyed film by giving them VIP seats and other perks. I had to conceal my annoyance at how these incidents took me away from larger concerns.

Our Italian counterparts working on the tour had the last laugh, though. I will never forget one of them, David Zarr. He loved to push my buttons, but he did so in such a jovial and effusive way that I couldn't stay mad at him for long. For example, one time he breached our no sponsor policy. Although Fiat was a sponsor, Bill didn't want to see any advertising for Fiat anywhere, as per our contract. I got to the stadium around 4 a.m. and saw a giant Fiat sculpture made of flowers that wasn't supposed to be there. I started considering how I could get rid of it before Bill caught wind, but wasn't quick enough. As soon as Bill saw it, he had a conniption fit. He took off running and screaming. When he got to the base of the sculpture, he started hacking away at it with his hands until it toppled over. Seething, he then demanded that the remnants of the sculpture be taken away and abruptly left. David had made a really stupid choice that was a waste of time, money, and energy, but that didn't affect me or the work I had left to do. As people rushed in to clean up the mess, I shrugged and moved to my next task.

Several months later, a large shipment arrived at my home. David Zarr had sent me fifty bootlegged, commemorative books about the Torino concert with unauthorized photos of the whole event.[2] On page sixty-seven, there was a half-page photo of me rocking a pearl necklace, sunglasses, and Finney plaits, looking pissed. The photographer had

---

2. See *I Rolling Stones in Italia*.

been able to get their photos after all. I gave all the books away but one. All those times that David promised us he would not break our rules, he was preparing the biggest "fuck you" he could. But it was a fuck you wrapped in love. I could only laugh. In the end, Italy is my favorite country. I sometimes feel like an Italian from Kansas.

While most of my memories of the Torino concerts revolved around our Italian counterparts and their shenanigans, in Torino I also learned that Keith Richards had a real beef with me. Since I'd started working, in my opinion, he had never been warm toward me and sometimes seemed downright cold. I never learned the impetus for his animosity. I figured it was because I was Mick's right-hand person and he didn't understand it. Maybe he thought I shouldn't have been as good at my job as I was. Perhaps this friction was a symptom of Keith and Mick's relationship. They could produce the most amazing music together one moment and then be at each other's throats the next. They had known each other since primary school and behaved more like pig-headed brothers than as long-time friends. But whatever was going on with Keith, I wasn't going to let it get in the way of the job I needed to do.

Before the second Torino concert, I was in the underground part of the stadium at my table where I kept the VIP passes. This subterranean room was a dark and dank place, but it impressed me with its understated magnificence. It was sort of tucked away, like a wine cellar. It was my sanctuary, where I could experience a calm before the storm that hit whenever the Stones took the stage.

The VIP passes were flown in every day from Bill Graham Presents in San Francisco, so that they couldn't be forged. As the only person allowed with the passes, I had set up shop in a corner of a small, quiet room and was absent-mindedly stamping them to add that last mark of authenticity. There were just a few of the crew in there getting ready for the show. I was listening to some chatter on my walkie-talkie when, all of a sudden, I heard the unmistakable voice of Keith behind me, "You stay out of my way, you fuckin' bitch."

I lost it. Keith had harassed me before and I wasn't going to stand for it any longer. I threw down my things and turned to face him. "You motherfucker, you're standing all the way over there." I wasn't known to curse, so I think that surprised some of the onlookers as much as my standing up to Keith had. But if you were ever to be taken seriously as a woman in this business, you had to become adept at the well-placed expletive. I then sneered, "If you are so fucking bad, do something!"

Keith threw off his blue mirrored sunglasses and as he lurched at me from the entry way, probably to berate me some more, Joe Seabrook—another Green Beret who was assigned to Keith because he was so volatile—intercepted.

I closed the door and caught my breath. *What did he mean "fuckin' bitch"? I was a woman. Ain't nobody's bitch.* Most of the time I didn't think about how I was one of three women out of a 250-person road crew. Most of the guys had so much respect for us. Their reputations for bedding anyone with a skirt may have been true, but in our working environment, our gender didn't seem to matter, because they knew when they saw us, we meant business. Paige Kevin, who was cool as a cookie and who ran logistics and Jan Simmons, who had the charm and wit to handle any situation—and who was practically Bill's human computer—could roll with anything. Meanwhile, I had spent half of my youth sleeping with a knife under my pillow. My shield was so deep that no one could break through. No man would ever lay a hand on me and survive.

I had no problem navigating these hypermasculine spaces as a woman, because the contract I negotiated each year was my code of ethics. Whatever the rider said needed to be done, it got done. I purposefully separated myself from everyone else so that there would be no mistaking that I meant business. For instance, I still made sure that my room wasn't on the same floor as everyone else. Bill used to say about me, "if you don't see her, she's in her room, because she only means business." This meant a lot coming from Bill, as right before I was set to go on the road with the Stones for the first time, Mick stopped by my place to warn me that Bill didn't want me in a position that no woman had held. Bill had said to Mick, "You're going to have someone who looks like that on the road with all those men? Are you crazy?"

But Mick, who is one of the most perceptive people I have ever met, knew the type of person that I was and he knew that I could handle 250 men on the road by myself. Mick ended up becoming my biggest champion in that regard. For example, one day, I had accompanied Mick to Los Angeles because he and Jack Nicholson were discussing a possible film collaboration. As we were being driven, I was in the front seat because I always insisted on sitting in next to the driver. The two men were discussing business in the back, when it suddenly got quiet. I heard Jack whisper something to Mick, and Mick responded loudly enough for me to hear, "Oh, forget about it. She's untouchable." I felt so proud of and grateful to Mick for vocally defending my job and my purpose. That's how I was able to be on the road with all these guys. I treated everyone the way that I wanted to be treated, but I was untouchable.

Outsiders always seemed surprised when my behind-the-scenes dynamic did not fit their expectations. When the German magazine *Stern* was conducting an interview with Mick, the reporter asked him about having a Black woman tour manager.

Mick responded, "Is she Black?" He effectively shut down the line of questioning. While I know that Mick was very attuned to questions of race—having made a whole career off incorporating Black musical traditions and even writing some lyrics that purportedly told the experiences of Black people—it was nice to know that Mick saw me as a person first and foremost. That was what I always wanted from the world, even though I seldom got it.

While I was still seething at Keith's verbal attack and the violence that he threatened before he was subdued, I heard a knock on the door. Someone had called Bill on the walkie talkie, even though he would never leave the stage from five a.m. until the show was over. This, apparently, was an emergency.

Bill opened the door and grabbed me by my shoulders. "Do you want a Valium?" he asked.

"No," I replied. "You know my no drug policy."

"How about some brandy?"

I nodded and he sent someone away to get me a glass. He then asked if I wanted to take the rest of the day off. I looked at him if he were crazy. He then smiled and went on his way while I kept doing my job and tried not to think about what had transpired.

When the band went on stage, I was standing behind the scenes with all the VIP passes. Keith came through and as he ran up the stairs, he glared at me and continued on. A few days later, when we were in Basel, Switzerland, I was on Keith's floor for a reason that I can't recall. Keith and Ronnie usually stayed on their own floor so they could keep the music loud. They wanted to think they were at a rock concert at all times. I headed down the corridor and as I turned the corner, I saw Keith walking toward me. As we passed each other, he said, "Next time, I'll get you," and smiled. I thought to myself, *You will never get me, Keith. I've put up with way worse than you in my life.* It turned out that he never bothered me again.

I tried to stay out of any personal issues, especially because things could be volatile within the group. However, I was still Mick's personal business liaison, so whenever he called on me for something, I was right by his side. When we arrived in Paris, we had a bit of downtime and he asked if I would accompany him on some important business. He didn't tell me what it was about but impressed upon me how he could really use some support.

We entered a Vietnamese restaurant and sat at a table close to the door so that Mick could watch everyone who entered. That's when he decided to come clean and confess that we were there to meet his daughter Karis for the first time. Karis was Mick's firstborn child, born to Marsha Hunt, the star of the musical *Hair* in the late '60s.

"Oh no, you tricked me! You know my rule. I don't get involved in personal business." I glared at him. We never hung out, so I didn't understand why he wanted me to be there for this most intimate of family events. Looking guilty, perhaps for dragging me into that, or perhaps for his past treatment of his daughter, he kept saying how he hoped that he would recognize her. Shortly after, a beautiful girl with an impressive mane of hair walked in. She was only twelve or so at the time, but she was almost as tall as I was. She came over to the table and she and Mick grabbed each other in a long embrace. He introduced me as she sat down. She was so astute and lady-like, wise beyond her years.

Everything seemed so relaxed considering the circumstances. They started talking, focusing mainly on her education since they were both whip-smart and studious—he used what he learned during his time at the London School of Economics to become a shrewd businessman, and she would graduate from Yale one day. This encounter was the beginning of a close-knit relationship, where throughout the years they learned to rely on each other. While Jerry had her faults, I learned later that she was the one who made Mick start taking responsibility for all his children. She began a tradition where his children, regardless of who their mother was, would spend time together during the summer. Many of the half-siblings became close. Meanwhile, Mick slowly transformed into a devoted father.

The European Tour was a huge success, but one of my favorite moments was when the work I did behind the scenes led to an opportunity to meet Princess Diana. I received a message from Sarah Marks, one of the women who worked in the London office, that Buckingham Palace was trying to reach me. Princess Di really wanted to meet the Stones, but, as a princess, she was not allowed to meet them in public. When I told the Stones, they were blown away. A series of meetings with both the Stones' security and Palace security finally paid off.

Everything played out like a movie. When we arrived at the palace, we were escorted into a decadent room, where the Stones and several other musicians and singers were lined up along the wall. I wasn't in the line to meet Princess Di, but I still wore a beloved Fabrice dress. Since I was his sample size and he loved to give me his creations, I always had a dress for every occasion. Princess Di entered and met all the band members one by one. She carried herself with such poise, grace and remarkable candor that I was blown out of my socks (or would have been, had I been wearing any). She then bowed her head deferentially to me from across the room. I couldn't believe that I had been involved in putting this moment together. Her passing was one of the saddest days of my life.

The tour ended as quickly as it began. Each band member went their separate way. No one knew it then, but there wouldn't be another Stones tour for seven years. Keith and Mick's relationship devolved as part of their cyclical ebb and flow and Mick decided to strike out on his own for a while. The media had a field day with this alleged treason, so it was hard for him to get good press for his solo venture. I honestly don't believe that he had plans to leave the band for good. He just had some creative threads that he wanted to pull and thought it was a good time.

I was surprised when he asked me if I wanted to coordinate his solo album, which meant organizing everything. I was occupying a producer role even though I was placed in the acknowledgements instead of the credits. Who knows what behind-the-scenes discussions led to that decision? In the end though, what mattered was that an album I worked on went platinum. Hanging proudly on my wall, my platinum record for *She's the Boss*, which has my name etched on the front, is one of my prized possessions. It signaled to me that perhaps there was a future music career lying dormant in me. Mick also marked the occasion by giving me a leather jacket with "She's the Boss" stitched on the lapel and a patch of the iconic Stones symbol sewn on the sleeve. I really was my own boss.

Chapter 8: Bill Graham Presents

Fig. 14. Signed photo of Bill Graham and Alvenia Bridges.
Original by Ken Regan. By Maya Angela Smith.

*This photo of Alvenia and Bill locked in a gaze is Alvenia's favorite.
It sits at eye level next to her desk, so that all she has to do is turn her
chair slightly to bask in both the image and his kind, inspirational words
to her. Ken Regan, whose photography documented musical greats such as
Jimi Hendrix, Bob Dylan, the Beatles, Bruce Springsteen, and the Rolling
Stones, was a constant fixture on any tour involving Bill Graham. While
Regan's lens was always trained on the big names, he had an uncanny sense
for knowing when to capture the special moments of the people behind the
scenes who made it possible for these big acts to shine. For him to photograph*

this private moment between Alvenia and Bill, which occurred right after Bill commended her for being "fucking bad," meant the world to her because the photo shows just how much he respected her.

There were two men in my life whose compassion and generosity helped me truly understand how wonderful humans could be. The first was, of course, John Von Neumann, and the second was Bill Graham. Even though they couldn't have been more different personality-wise, each of them saw me for me and treated me the way I deserved to be treated.

While Chuck Berry may have been the godfather of rock and roll, Bill Graham revolutionized how we consumed rock music, evolving the industry in unimaginable ways. He was a visionary who was never satisfied with the status quo, so he constantly pushed himself and those around him. A veritable force to be reckoned with, his kicking down the Fiat display at the Stones concert in Torino was just the tip of the iceberg. I will never forget how he eviscerated Barry Fey—a promotor in Denver—when I was working with U2 on the *Joshua Tree* tour. Since the Stones were not together for most of the eighties, I spent my time helping Bill Graham with his multiple endeavors. My experience with U2 was delightful. They had a different energy than other groups and were always so appreciative of the little things, like when I made backstage look like a desert, with a huge cactus as the main attraction. While U2 and I enjoyed a friendly working relationship, Barry Fey and Bill Graham were laboring under a much more antagonistic one.

At 4:00 a.m. the worker bees, those of us responsible for making sure concerts actually happened, would start our shifts. Every morning, Bill was right there with us, checking that we had everything that we needed. The crew would eat breakfast backstage and Bill would go over the stage to ensure that it was up to his standards. You could always tell when Bill was nearby because the index cards that hung around his neck—strategically, so that his hands could be free—would emit a dull slapping sound as he buzzed from location to location.

I happened to be passing by one fateful morning when he suddenly called me over. Bill then stepped back and turned a table of food upside down. As people stopped what they were doing to stare in an uneasy mixture of shock and expectation, Bill went to the next table and turned it upside down. He methodically turned every table upside down, one by one, as bits of food went flying and utensils came crashing down. I knew I was going to be needed, so I just stood by and watched.

Bill looked at me and said, "Get Barry Fey." So, I went in search of Barry Fey. When I found him, I told him that Bill would like to see him.

"Where is he? I will be there in a minute," Barry replied, unaware of the wrath that would soon descend upon him.

"No, it's now. I promise you, it's now."

You didn't want Bill to come looking for you, especially when you messed with his crew. At that point, Barry started to look nervous, since the two of them had always had a contentious relationship.

As soon as we arrived, Bill glowered at Barry and said, "Smell it." He then walked away. Barry was trembling slightly as he bent down to smell the food. He must've already known that the food was rotten, since it had sat out in the heat for so long. For this infraction, Bill made mincemeat out of Barry Fey. In return, the crew received their non-rotten, replacement food in no time.

Bill's childhood, a winding story of escape and reinvention, was even more fraught than mine. Bill—born Wulf Wolodia Grajonca—never knew his father, a Russian immigrant in Berlin, because he died two days after Bill's birth. Bill then lost his mother when she placed him and his youngest sister, Tolla, in an orphanage that sent Jewish children to France in exchange for Christian ones, because of the increasing danger that Jews faced in 1930s Nazi Germany. Two years later, when France's Vichy government paved the way for the German occupation of France, Bill and Tolla were on the move again, marching through France with sixty-two other children. By the time Bill finally reached Marseilles, his sister Tolla, having been weakened by months of malnutrition, had already died of pneumonia.

Bill was one of the lucky eleven children who survived the odyssey that would eventually land them in New York on September 24, 1941. He had survived against the odds; however, the agony of waiting nine weeks before being chosen by a foster family—the last of the eleven children to find a home—was something that he never forgot. The feeling of being unwanted, coupled with the news of his mother's murder—she was gassed on her way to Auschwitz—was the lowest moment of his life. I thought that I knew what rejection, hate and heartache looked like, but nothing could prepare me for the sheer horror that overcame me when Bill shared his childhood. However, just like me, Bill was a fighter and he used those ghastly moments as the fuel that would drive him throughout his life.[1]

I will never forget when we were on tour with the Stones in Vienna. It must have been early July of 1982, because Jerry, who had joined us on tour, and I had July birthdays—only a few days apart. Bill invited the executive touring party for a birthday celebration dinner at a restaurant

---

1. For more on Bill Graham, see his biography by the Bill Graham Memorial Foundation.

owned by two of his surviving sisters, Sonja and Ester. He had bought them the property, because it was the site of the concentration camp in which they had been imprisoned during the war. As he stood there in his Armani suit telling us their family history, I got goosebumps.

A few years later, the Bill Graham Presents offices were firebombed in San Francisco, in retaliation for a rally he had sponsored in Union Square. He was protesting a visit by President Ronald Reagan to a German cemetery that housed the remains of SS officers. Bill was constantly using his clout to call attention to injustice and to the whitewashing of history. While Bill was able to recover his businesses after this destructive attack, he lost a lot of important memorabilia in the explosion and subsequent burning.

Again, he used the hatred and vitriol directed at him simply for being Jewish and a Holocaust survivor as motivation to put on numerous charity events. Bill used his connections and money to bring the biggest names to his charity endeavors, such as his "Conspiracy of Hope" tour commemorating Amnesty International's twenty-five years of protecting human rights or his "Human Rights Now!" tour in '88 celebrating the 40th anniversary of the Universal Declaration of Human Rights.

It was, therefore, not surprising that Bill was responsible for presenting Nelson Mandela with a packed Oakland Coliseum in the summer of 1990. Over 60,000 people cheered for the recently freed political prisoner—having only left Robben Island four months prior—as he toured the world to drum up support for the anti-apartheid movement. Oakland was the last leg of this successful tour. I had the honor of meeting Mandela a couple of weeks earlier in New York City when I was helping Bill with that portion of Mandela's tour. Even though Bill ended up pulling out of the event at Yankee Stadium because of political infighting among the different constituents in charge, his initial involvement afforded me the opportunity of a lifetime. As Mandela greeted me, I bowed, and he took my hand and just held it. The transfer of energy was electric. This man had suffered twenty-seven years in prison for fighting for freedom, equality, and justice. He knew the worst of humankind and yet, he harbored no ill will. In fact, he emitted so much love, that there was no space for negativity. Even though he had such a tough task before him—freeing Black South Africa—he did so with an equanimity that only serious soul-searching and forgiveness could provide. I was in Mandela's presence for just a moment before I had to run off and get back to work, but it was life changing. I also got to meet his teenage grandson who accompanied Mandela on his tour. He showed up unexpectedly at my apartment as the guest of one of my friends. I remember sitting on the couch with him, as he asked me who all the people that I had enshrined on my wall were. Before he left, he signed a corner of my wall.[2]

⤜⟶·❀·⟵⤛

While Bill occasionally handled speaking engagements such as Mandela's, most of his charity events were full-scale concerts. One of these events was a concert for peace and nuclear disarmament on July 4, 1987, in Moscow.

Bill called me up a few weeks prior and asked, "Alvenia, would you like to go to Russia?"

---

2. For more information on Mandela's visit to New York, see McShane "Nelson Mandela."

I said, "Sure, Bill, but what is this about?"

In an even tone that belied how much work would be involved to pull this event off, he explained, "I want to do something big for the culmination of the two-week Soviet-American peace walk happening between Leningrad and Moscow. I've got James Taylor, Bonnie Raitt, Santana, the Doobie Brothers, and Hall & Oates on board."

I interrupted him, "Bill, where are you now?"

"I'm in Moscow." He then detailed how the Soviet Peace committee was co-sponsoring the peace walk and was also in charge of convincing Soviet bands to perform. Bill had secured almost $600,000 from Apple co-founder Steve Wozniak and was now in turbo-drive trying to get all the necessary arrangements together to pull it off. He then listed all the things I needed to do, the most daunting of which was to get rushed visas for all the performers and technicians, from a country with which we had been engaged in a decades-old cold war. I was a little taken aback, composing myself before asking my next question, "How am I going to do this, Bill?"

He simply responded, "Their management people are waiting for your call. You'll figure out the rest."

Bill would often come to me when he needed help with seemingly insurmountable tasks for his grandiose projects. His faith in me to do the right thing, while often nerve-racking, had such a freeing effect. I had spent a lifetime with no guidance—stemming from the lack of parental support in my childhood—so a lot of my life consisted of me figuring out what needed to be done. The lack of instruction had made me very adept at problem-solving and troubleshooting, but because I did not have the pedigree or the traditional training for many of the predicaments I ended up in, most people underestimated me. Ever since that moment on the moving sidewalk, Bill had made it clear that he had the utmost faith in me and knew that if he gave me something to do, it would get done, and done well. Thinking about his trust and respect always provided a wonderful feeling.

That feeling was non-existent after his phone call, however, as I scrambled to corral some of the biggest musicians of the era. While he was in Moscow, I was in charge of the musicians' logistics—airfare, visas, food, you name it. The musicians and crew totaled over sixty-five people. We all flew to D.C. from different parts of the country and caught our connecting flight to Moscow on a chartered flight by Aeroflot, which we affectionately called Aeroslot. Miraculously, everyone scheduled to perform in Moscow made it.

The whole experience was surreal. All the musicians were staying in Moscow, but I had a room in a hotel outside of town, complete with my own female Soviet guard who stood outside my door at all times. I still don't know if she was there to keep me in or keep others out. The venue itself was unlike any I had ever worked. Troops encircled the stadium and security officers walked the grounds during the six-hour concert, as American and Soviet bands performed. The spectators near the stage seemed to really enjoy the music, although they were definitely more moved by the Russian folk music, than the American rock music. The 20,000 or so audience members in the stands were less engaged, probably because they could barely see anything. Furthermore, we were unable to convince our Soviet counterparts to distribute most of the tickets to people who actually liked American Rock music. Worried that young fans would be harder to control, the authorities wanted to limit their numbers. The Soviet Union had been closed off for so long. This concert was a baby step in opening relations with the US.

While the reception was more subdued than most rock concerts I had put on, pulling off a successful concert was a huge feat. We had been able to work effectively with the Soviet Union. The Soviet government had approved all the rushed visa applications and allowed all our musical and stage equipment to pass through the Polish border with ease. They didn't even seem too annoyed when Bill made arrangements with Hungary to bring us food every day by plane. He used his own money so we could eat Vienna sausages and other delights to diversify the food options.

Just when I thought that the show had been relatively tame, an unexpected event occurred during our return home. I met the performers at the airport in Moscow and everyone was acting weird. One person was even sitting on the floor with a paper bag over his head. Getting people on the plane was like herding cats. Turns out that most of them had tripped on acid in the Red Square before going to the airport. That was one of the strangest flights I've ever been on. I guess something could be said for the fact that most of them were going to San Francisco.[3]

While this concert for nuclear disarmament was a logistical nightmare, nothing compared to Live Aid in July of 1985. Bill was always a sight to see during events, as he was continually huffing and puffing and yelling at everyone. But he was particularly worked up about Live Aid because it was something that had never been done before. When Irish singer-songwriter Bob Geldof and Scottish musician Midge Ure ap-

---

3. For more information about this concert, see "July 4 Rock Concert for Peace."

proached Harvey Goldsmith in the UK and Bill in the US and explained their vision of a dual-venue benefit concert that would raise money and awareness for the humanitarian crisis in Ethiopia, there was initially disbelief. We would need to rely on new technology to not only simulcast live performances around the world, but to essentially merge two concerts into one, with the performers at Wembley Stadium in the UK beginning the sixteen-hour extravaganza and then passing the torch to their counterparts at JFK stadium in Philadelphia. The performances would alternate between the UK and the US for part of the show. There were even plans for an intercontinental duet between Mick Jagger and David Bowie that ended up being pre-recorded because of synchronization issues.

In addition to the massive logistical feat, many performers were uninterested at first. They didn't understand the concept. This was before benefit concerts were a common occurrence. Some of the musicians were moved by the images of how this famine affected human lives. Others only wanted to join after they realized what a huge event this would be. Bill spent the first part of the planning trying to convince people to participate and then the last couple of weeks turning people down, including those he had reached out to earlier, because we were overbooked. Bill knew that some bridges would be burned, but he didn't see any way to accommodate everyone, even after extending the concert by several hours.

Bill was also quite worried about the lack of Black representation slated to perform. Bob Geldof had secured several major acts but none of them were Black. Bill tried to rectify this by contacting everyone he knew, but the biggest Black performers at the time had prior engagements and turned him down. In the end, he relied on Larry Magid, who was based in Philadelphia and well connected to major Black musical acts. Through Larry, we signed on people like the Four Tops, Teddy Pendergrass, Ashford and Simpson, and Patti Labelle. Separately, we were able to get Tina Turner, who had showed her support early in the planning stages.

Other issues revolved around what do you do when you have so many massive personalities sharing a stage? The sheer number of acts was astounding and when you added all the fame and notoriety present in such a small space, you can imagine what it was like. People vied for the best time slots and were upset when they couldn't play as long as they wanted. There was even jostling for physical space, like when Madonna's entourage moved Eric Clapton out of the way so she could walk by unimpeded.

Against the chaotic backdrop of Live Aid, Ken Regan, an incredibly sweet person and a fantastic photographer who had snapped iconic images of heavyweights such as Bob Dylan, the Beatles, the Stones, and Hendrix, approached me about three hours before the US portion of the concert was to start. Wearing his usual khaki ensemble and a huge smile, he said, "Alvenia, if you can get all these people together for a group photo, we could have the cover of *People* magazine." He then rattled off the list of people like Tina Turner, Bob Dylan, and Madonna.

"Ken, I'll kill you for asking me something like this," I said.

He laughed. "Thanks, Alvenia. There's a tent already set up. Just bring everyone over there."

I was a big fan of Ken, so even though I was in the middle of mayhem and had a laundry list of tasks to complete, I started running from tent to tent. Miraculously, people said yes with little hesitation. Madonna's people were a little tough because it was almost showtime, but they eventually agreed. Tina Turner, on the other hand, was the most kind. When I passed by her trailer, I ran into her manager Roger Davies, who knew right away that Tina would say yes. That's just who she is, always finding time for people and good causes. However, he asked me to wait while he confirmed with her.

As I waited, I remembered how a few years prior, I had met Tina for the first time. It must have been either 1979 or 1980. I was going from Paris to Los Angeles and Thierry Mugler—a designer from my modeling days whose bold forms and colors I always found captivating—said to me, "Darling, I want to give you a gift, but could you do me a favor in return?" He proceeded to give me three versions of the same dress. Mine was in red. The other two were for Diana Ross and Tina Turner. I couldn't believe the task he set out for me. For one, they were my idols. I didn't know what I would say to them if I ever met them. Two, he had no contact info for them. He said, "Consider it a challenge!"

When I got to Los Angeles, I tried to find out who their agents were. When I got in touch with Diana Ross's management, they weren't very accommodating. I ended up dropping it off at their offices and hoped that it wouldn't get "lost." With regards to Tina, I got in touch with Roger, who was so amenable and sweet. When he heard back from Tina, he informed me that Tina wanted me to bring the dress to her home. I asked if I could just drop it off, because I knew I would be starstruck if I met her in person. Not only was this before I really became entrenched in the music business and was used to meeting the biggest names on earth, but I also just had so much respect for her because of her courage and tenacity. She was a hero to me.

Tina insisted that I visit her and when I realized I couldn't get out of this, I relented. We arranged a time to meet and as usual, I arrived at least an hour early. Since I was a terrible driver and therefore crept down the side streets very slowly, I always planned for way more time than anyone should need. I parked up the hill and waited. When it was just about sundown, I made my way up the path. Similar butterflies as those when I went up the path to John's door all those years ago took flight in my stomach. The setting was so similar. Tina had a tall wooden fence and bells hung everywhere. She was Buddhist with an aesthetic to match. As soon as I reached the door, a beautiful Asian woman dressed in all white bowed to me. I had planned to give the dress to whomever answered so I wouldn't have to meet Tina, but as I listened to the water flowing down the indoor waterfall, an overwhelming sense of calm washed over me. The house was filled with such positive energy. A few minutes after my arrival, Tina emerged in white pajamas and thanked me for bringing Thierry's gift. She then invited me to stay for dinner. I told her I couldn't—with the way I drove, if I left too late, I wouldn't make it home until the morning—so she requested that I at least stay for a drink. When she asked what I wanted, I said, "I'll have whatever you're having."

As we visited, she spoke about spirituality and finding kindness in every person. She gushed about how wonderful a person Thierry was. She philosophized about how she navigated the world, whether things were going well or badly. She was so serene. I couldn't imagine she was the same person who had endured such turmoil at the hands of her ex-husband, had to rely on food stamps after their divorce and had to rebuild her career from the ground up.[4] She told me that while it was sometimes hard to keep faith when so many people appeared to relish in harming others, we had to allow ourselves to trust people or we would spend life being lonely, bitter, and inhuman. I don't know how she knew what I needed to hear at that point in my life, but she did. She spoke to my soul. I took her words to heart and promised I would put her advice deep in myself.

Years later, back at Live Aid, as I was cherishing that memory, Tina stuck her head out of the trailer, catapulting me back to the present. Exuding her usual warmth, she told me she would love to do the photo. She then added that it was good to see me again. I couldn't believe she remembered who I was.

So, Ken took the photo he wanted (a copy of which he sent to me) and he got it published on the cover of *People* magazine. I went back to running around like crazy, doing the other 99 things on my list. At one point, I snuck a peek at Mick and Tina, who were the only ones who got to rehearse because they were doing something together for the first time. It was surreal watching them perform to an empty stadium only moments before it would be teeming with people. Then, right before their duet started, Mick asked for my skintight black and green spandex pants. I was confused but was happy to oblige because I had another outfit in my bag. During their performance, the crowd went wild when Mick ripped off Tina's skirt and she spun around in nothing but a leotard. Having seen the rehearsal, I was expecting it. What I was not expecting was seeing Mick do his own wardrobe change mid

---

4. Tina Turner chronicles her life story in several books, including her most recent memoir *My Love Story*.

performance. He switched from his flowing lavender pants to *my* pants in front of everyone. Those pants were immortalized on stage. Too bad I only ever saw them again in photos.[5]

To pull off something like Live Aid took an enormous amount of time, work, and energy. Even though I think Bill was proud of the work he had done to put it on, you wouldn't have known just by looking at him. He always had a dour presence exacerbated by his lack of sleep. Only occasionally, could you experience Bill when he was relatively relaxed. One of my favorite Bill moments was being his date for the first ever Rock and Roll Hall of Fame induction ceremony at the Waldorf-Astoria in 1986.

He had called me out of the blue and said, "Hey sexy lady, it's the sexy Jew from San Francisco. I'm coming in town today. Get a dress, as I have quite the night planned." This line was how our nights on the town always began.

Always up for a surprise, I rushed to get ready for the evening. I went to my favorite designer, Fabrice, who said, "Darling, take this one," and handed me a sequined gray beauty of an evening dress. I promised to bring it back, but he smiled, "Oh, keep it, darling."

Bill picked me up and we headed to what would be a lavish ceremony and reception. Some of the biggest names in music history were being inducted that night, including Elvis, James Brown, Little Richard, Ray

---

5. For another first-hand account of Live Aid, see Jones's "Live Aid 1985."

Charles, and Sam Cooke. The list went on. I was seated next to inductee Chuck Berry, who had me in stitches as he complained about how bored he was. I definitely found the event much more exciting than he did, as I had been able to speak with a great deal of musical legends. Bill seemed genuinely happy. His normally intense stare—the result of working multiple calculations in his head—was absent for once. The night was such a whirlwind of magic that I don't even remember how I got home and out of that dress. I woke up the next morning high on life.

However, of all the amazing concerts he made happen and all the charity events he made thrive, I think Bill Graham was most proud of his toughest feat: reconciling with his son David. Work took him away from his family very often and he couldn't spend as much time with them as he wanted. Despite major personal and career setbacks—such as when the Stones did not hire Bill to promote their *Steel Wheels* Tour—Bill was trying to correct some major mistakes he had made in his life. Most importantly, he wanted to ensure that David would see him as the father he had failed to be. Therefore, in 1989, Bill threw David a 21st birthday party that he would never forget.

He flew in everyone who worked for Bill Graham Presents in San Francisco so that they could all celebrate with them. I was in charge of logistics. Bill took over the Circle Line Cruises that circumnavigated Manhattan, so that we could see the city from different angles. Before joining the rest of the party, Bill chartered a helicopter to fly him and David from upstate New York. They made a stop on Ellis Island and Bill showed David where he landed in America after escaping Nazi extermination. Bill then took us to his favorite restaurant where he gave us T-shirts adorned on the front with a black-and-white photo of a young

David with his hands on his hips looking fierce. On the back were the words "I'm twenty-one now! Don't mess wit' me!"

At one point, I caught Bill's eye and he smiled at me. He then turned his attention back to David and just beamed with pride. Here was a man who had his family ripped apart because of one of the worst atrocities this world has ever known. Then, his own fervor to make a successful career from absolutely nothing caused him to sacrifice a healthy family life. He spent so much of his life alone and lonely, but now, there was some redemption as he proudly took on his father role. Some relationships could be mended.

Chapter 9: The Spirit Moves Through Words and Music

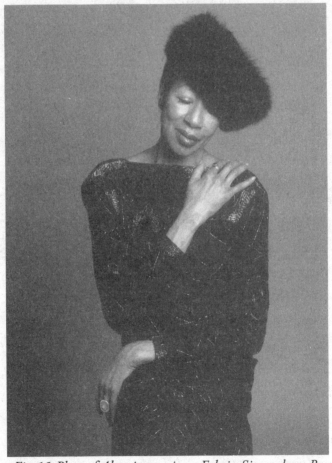

Fig. 15. Photo of Alvenia wearing a Fabrice Simon dress. By Kate Simon. Used with permission.

Fig. 16. Xerox of photo of Alvenia at Nick Ashford and Valerie Simpson's White Party. Original by unknown.

The first time I saw this photo of Alvenia (Fig. 15) enveloped in a Fabrice Simon dress, I was moved by the serenity on her face. She always tells me how wonderful she feels when his creations touch her body. After all, she was his sample size and this dress looks as if it were made for her. She wears it with the same ease as the plush hat that crowns her head. To this day, no one can wear a hat like she can. I also can't help but notice how one's eye is drawn to her long, strong hands—a perfect pinnacle to her flowing arms. The noxious venom that Alvenia's mother spewed about her body and its "orangutan" proportions no longer retains its sting. Alvenia has learned that she is beautiful and embodies it in the way that she carries herself. She no longer pays heed to those who make her feel that she isn't worth it.

Alvenia doesn't remember who took the second photo (Fig. 16), but it is special to me because it was the catalyst for Alvenia granting me a peek into her extraordinary past. Of all the photos on the wall—photos of Jimi Hendrix, Bob Marley, Roberta Flack, the list goes on—this was the one that first grabbed my attention because it was the only one that centers Alvenia. She is positioned in a way that conveys her commanding yet understated presence and thus best illustrates who Alvenia is. As the central figure connected in various ways to those around her, I also get a sense of the myriad relational experiences through which she influences, and has been influenced by, various people throughout her life. As a candid photo, it highlights Alvenia's capacity for exuding great joy.

I credit rock and roll for expanding my horizons and opening myself up to the musical genius of some of the biggest names in the business. I learned how to manage shows for crowds of close to 200,000 people and when you think about productions such as Live Aid, I was involved in creating an experience that over 1.5 billion people enjoyed live. That was a third of the world's population at that time. During each concert, I would say to myself, "I get paid to do this!" Being on the road amidst all this energy was a constant high for me, because I was made for this fast-paced lifestyle. Life had started off so slowly and now I was surfing a Jetstream. But while my life behind the scenes of rock and roll had become such a huge part of who I was, I was still firmly grounded in the music of my roots.

With my little radio, my teenage self would bop around to a new phenomenon encompassing the airways: the Motown sound. Everything that made me really move my body was coming out of the Motor City. Tunes such as "Shop Around" and "Please Mr. Postman" heralded this new era. While we never had a TV to watch these singers perform their moves when I was growing up, I choreographed dances to each song while hiding out in my room. This music got me through one of the roughest patches of my life. I needed something other than school to help me keep my promise to Mama. Dancing to the radio redirected the energy that might have gone into killing Ed Madden the next time he touched my sister or into fighting some white person who insisted on attacking my humanity.

One of the most exhilarating moments was when I first heard little Stevie Wonder blowing up his harmonica with "Fingertips." At thirteen years old, he was the youngest to ever top the charts. I remember how my body would just let loose, undulating to Stevie's hypnotic riffs. I knew that little boy was going to take over the world with his abilities and penchant for tapping into your soul. So, when at 4:00 a.m. one morning in the mid-eighties I got a phone call with the voice on the other end singing "I Just Called to Say I Need You," I almost fell out of bed. When the phone first rang, I thought it was Bill Graham calling during his usual insomnia to go over details about upcoming events. But that silky smooth sound on the other end was nothing like Bill's gruff, to-the-point voice.

"Stevie Wonder," I said after he explained why he was calling. "Let me finish this tour I'm on and I'll get in touch with you as soon as I can."

True to my word, I went to Los Angeles to see him. However, as I was on route, I was growing out of sorts. I kept hearing stories about his entourage and so-called friends that surrounded him. People warned me that they were no good. I had spent most of my life only being guided by the little voice in my head that I called the Spirit. This time it kept telling me no and there were other signs supporting that little voice. At the airport, for instance, my bag with all my jewelry was swiped. On the drive to the studio, I narrowly escaped a major accident. I confided in a friend who told me to just come home because nothing was going right. But I convinced myself that I needed to see this through, even as everything was running amuck.

I ended up signing on with Stevie, basically because of his incredible soul. He was so loving and kind to everyone around him. How could I not support him? He used his gift for so much good. I'll never forget the time we went to a hospital in Detroit. He wanted to do a concert in the chapel for the staff—his way of thanking them for all the help they gave him as he managed his blindness as a child. He would also visit sick children and compose songs for them, a different song for each kid. They would light up when gifted their own special song. I was in tears more than once while on the road with Stevie.

The tears that Stevie elicited from me were because of his generous soul, but those weren't all I cried for. Watching people mistreat Stevie in all sorts of ways, brought on tears that came from a much darker place. The tour I was assisting him with was *In Square Circle;* I hum "Part-time Lover" to myself until this day. We should've been selling out, but we weren't. I saw no promoters. There was no real buzz surrounding him. Since I was in charge of making sure Stevie got everything in his rider, I knew he should be getting paid well. But I saw no evidence that any of that money was going to him. While the bodyguards wore high-flying clothes, flew first class and drove Rolls Royces, I watched in horror as a make-up artist cleaned Stevie's face with Seabreeze and stored his clothes in a black garbage bag. This was Stevie! Why were they treating him this way?

I made the difficult decision of parting ways with him after his New York show. While I adored Stevie, I couldn't accept his money while bearing witness to such callousness. I threw him a party at a new club my friend had opened. After the party, I went up to him, grabbed his hand and told him how sorry I was, but I was leaving.

When he asked why, I decided to be honest, "Stevie, it's these people around you. I can't watch the way they treat you. You deserve so much more. If I can't do anything to help fix it, I can't be here to witness it."

His reply broke my heart, "What am I supposed to do? This is who I have."

I thought about those who had treated me like dirt and how I left them without ever looking back. The world was a lonely place without supporters by your side. But was it worth keeping around people who had no respect for you, who only asked what they could take from you and never thought about what they could give? Stevie had made his decision a long time ago. Nothing I said would ever change his mind. It made me so sad, but I respected him for his loyalty even if it caused him pain. Stevie could see better than anyone in the world. He knew what he was doing.

A while later, the husband-and-wife songwriting duo Nickolas Ashford and Valerie Simpson opened a restaurant and I ran into Stevie there. I approached him to say hello. Stevie would always recognize my perfume and turn toward me with his brilliant smile, even when I was still feet away. This time, however, when he caught my scent, he turned his back to me. It was one of the most soul-crushing experiences of my life. I assume he thought I had abandoned him. If only he knew how untrue that was. I think of him all the time. Stevie will always have a place in my heart.

This experience with Stevie made me realize how important it was to trust the Spirit. I had become adept at listening to it when it was guiding me into a new adventure and removing obstacles from my path, but when it would caution me to slow down or suggest I avoid an opportunity, I'd always been hardheaded. It sometimes took me more than once to learn a lesson. The lesson resurfaced when I refused to listen to the Spirit years later.

By the early 2000s, I had not worked for a while, having pretty much removed myself from the music industry after Bill Graham's abrupt passing in 1991—something I haven't gotten over until this day. I sometimes thought about re-entering the business but never heavily considered it until Patti LaBelle approached me.

There was much I liked about Patti. Her music was great. She was no-nonsense like me and didn't take any bull from anyone. She had suffered more family tragedy than a person ever should and I could relate to some of the horrors she endured. She grew up in a physically abusive household and was sexually molested by a family friend when she was twelve. She then lost family member after family member in what could be considered a cruel joke. In the span of fifteen years, she watched all three of her sisters succumb to cancer and mourned the passing of both her parents as well. With everyone around her dying, she didn't think she would live past fifty. Furthermore, her crumbling love life compounded the pain. After a tumultuous marriage, she separated from her husband/manager in the late nineties. When she came to me, she was trying to figure out how to move forward.[1]

Patti was a fighter and I admired her deeply for that. When she visited me and told me how she wanted me to help her get her life together, I felt compelled to provide whatever assistance I could. She was already well established, so it would be an honor to help her rise even higher. However, at the same time, there was that voice again, gnawing on the back of my mind, telling me that this wasn't my place, this wasn't where I should be. But just like with Stevie, I shut it out and moved forward.

Soon after, she called to say she wanted to have dinner with me. I made reservations at a little bistro around the corner and planned to walk over. She insisted on picking me up even when I tried to convince her otherwise. When she pulled up to the door of my building in her Hummer bedazzled with lights, I felt pangs of embarrassment spiking their way through my body. I have never been a flashy person and to have all my neighbors see me get into this monstrous vehicle, just to go around the corner, made me incredibly uncomfortable. As soon as I sat down, she sprung another surprise on me: "Sweetie, I have to go downtown just for a second to check out some kid from Philly I promised to see at his club."

I said, "Patti, we have a reservation. I'll wait right here."

She retorted, "Come on, Alvenia. Don't be so rigid." The only thing rigid about me at that moment was my conscience, which kept warning me about going. It knew something I didn't.

---

1. Patti Labelle provides insight into her life in her autobiography *Don't Block the Blessings*.

Her driver took us down to the garment district, which was generally quiet at night. We pulled up at a dingy little place where a tiny, dark opening led to some stairs. With each step I took, the Spirit was screaming at me not to go any further. I wanted to listen, but Patti kept begging me to follow her, so I just went along. Once we got to the top, which opened almost directly to the stage, I parked myself there. I've always been known for standing next to an exit, as I feel safer with a quick escape. She sighed when she realized I wouldn't go further and continued on toward the stage. As she made her way on stage, the crowd went wild. When she started singing "Lady Marmalade," the place erupted. A large man standing next to me wearing a tangerine sweater and sporting a football player physique lifted his arms in joy. In his euphoria, he accidentally knocked me backwards down the stairs, where I landed on my knee. I wasn't going to wait around for Patti to find out something was wrong. I hoisted myself up from the ground and miraculously, a cab pulled up as I exited the building.

As I settled into the cab, Patti came up to the window and started banging on it. I kept saying to the driver, 58th and 7th, 58th and 7th, 58th and 7th, and we sped away. The pain hadn't hit my knee yet, but I was definitely feeling woozy. Soon, I could see the deli at the corner of my block. The driver, a Sikh man who turned out to be a guardian angel when I realized I was without my purse and unable to pay him, jumped out the car to open my door. My buddy, a homeless Senegalese guy named Tony who was always perched at the corner with a sign that read "Everybody needs a little help some time" came running over when he saw the look on my face. Tony and the cab driver gently pulled me out of the car.

He then asked, "What happened, baby?"

"Please, just help me to the door," I replied. They helped me up the stairs. Then, the doorman took over since Tony wasn't allowed in the building and the cab driver had to return to his shift.

With the help of the doorman, I made it to my couch and propped my leg up. It was stiff, but the pain still hadn't started in earnest. By the time my roommate Larry arrived, I was screaming. He stayed up with me all night replenishing the bags of ice that rested on my knee. I was out of my mind with pain. I should've gone to the hospital immediately, but I kept thinking the pain would pass. Finally, I told Larry to call the ambulance.

My knee was swollen immensely, but they didn't see any major damage, so I was released even though the pain was beyond comprehension. I was without health insurance so the hospital probably figured they couldn't do much for me anyway. The physical pain has seesawed between dull and excruciating throughout the years, but it is the emotional pain that has left scars. I tried reaching out to Patti, not to expect anything from her, just so we could talk through it and move forward. I truly believe in letting go. But Patti refused to talk to me. She found out what had happened and changed all her numbers so I couldn't reach her. She even changed her super private number, the one she gave me when she wanted me to work with her. Her abandonment broke my heart. I had shown such interest in helping her and she had no problem with throwing me away. I decided to cut Patti off as well. I don't know if she ever had a change of heart because I made sure to never have contact with her again.

The physical pain was nothing compared to the psychological pain left by that fateful night. Each year, my knee got worse and worse. I lost some of my independence when I could no longer move freely and ably. Despite the amazing keepsakes and trinkets I've collected in my work and travel, my mobility has always been my prized possession. I was able to escape utter despair when I left Kansas. I was able to reach soaring heights when I made it to Europe. I was able to finally call a place home when I settled down in New York. My ability to cross borders and transcend boundaries had been the greatest gift ever bestowed on me. My legs have allowed me to dance my way out of depression, model high-end fashion, and run like a racehorse from task to task while on the road—but now my leg is a liability.

My experiences with Patti and Stevie were both examples of how I went against the Spirit and I consider it a spiritual embarrassment when I don't listen to that guiding voice inside me—the only guidance that has accompanied me throughout my life. When I have listened to the Spirit, it has shown me my path. It worked through Mama, Roberta, John and Bill in obvious ways. However, sometimes, the Spirit just throws someone wacky my way, someone whose presence offers such a refreshing change of pace, that you have to sit back and accept the ride. Miles Davis was such a person.

My story has interwoven with Miles's on numerous occasions throughout our lives. I often saw him in passing and knew him by association, such as through my quick encounter with Betty Mabry, Miles's wife for a brief time, whose glorious Afro I complimented when meeting her and Finney at the Whisky A-Go-Go in the 1960s. Miles was also around soon after I moved to New York the first time, when I was living with Johnny McLaughlin and near Tony Williams and Dave Holland, all musicians who played with Miles at different points in their careers. Miles and I also shared the same hairdresser, as Finney kept us both in style. While the world will always think of Miles as one of the biggest jazz pioneers ever to grace the stage, I will never forget him for his visual art.

Miles's love of art started after resorting to drawing and painting as a type of physical therapy upon recovering from a stroke that affected his ability to play music. Miles never did anything halfway. Once he realized his talent, he threw himself into this alluring form of creative expression. It offered a nice counterbalance to his music and he even incorporated his art into some of his album covers like *Amandla*. (Interesting side note: "Amandla," meaning "power" in Xhosa and Zulu, was the first word Mandela yelled to his followers as he emerged from prison. It became the rallying cry for the anti-Apartheid movement.) Miles's style evoked famous artists such as Basquiat and Picasso, but it had a distinctly Miles flavor that only a master of Jazz could create.

One evening in the early nineties, I got a call from Miles. You always knew it was Miles as soon as you picked up the phone. He asked me to come over to his place right away. He lived a block from me in the Essex and the back entrance was literally across the street from me. I arrived and took the elevator, which opened right into his apartment. Two of his friends were there and as I walked up between them, I spotted Miles painting at his easel with his back turned to us and Central Park before him out the window. I called out to Miles and asked him what he wanted.

He turned around, looked at me a bit confused and said, "I forgot." This exchange was not an unfamiliar scene.

I chuckled. "Okay Miles. I'm headed back home. If you remember anything, let me know."

As soon as I got home, the phone rang and Miles told me he remembered what he wanted to tell me. I made the trip back over to his place. Without waiting for me to speak, he grunted, "I want to put on a show."

"A show?" I inquired.

"Yes, of my artwork."

"When do you want this to happen?"

"Right away."

"Right away? I'll need some time to put it together."

"You have two weeks."

I cautiously agreed to take this on but wondered how to even start. The next morning, I called my friend Mary McDonald at *Rolling Stone* to see if she knew who I could contact about gallery space. Through her suggestions I approached the Nerlino gallery down on Greene Street. After Joanne Nerlino saw the sheer magnitude and utter mastery of Miles's work—in seven years he had created over 100 pieces of art—she was as excited as I was to share his talents with the masses. I went right to work on getting the word out.

Miraculously, the show ended up being a huge hit. As Miles surveyed his creations at the opening reception, I asked him how things were going. He turned to me with a huge grin and a throaty exclamation: "Timing is everything, bitch!" He was very pleased.[2]

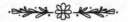

---

2. For more information, see Nerlino's "Visual Art of Miles Davis."

When the Spirit wanted to bring me excitement, it would send me Miles. When it wanted to remind me that things would be alright with the world, it would send me Ashford and Simpson. Nickolas Ashford and Valerie Simpson may be the most understated musicians in American musical history. While their singing careers never took off on a large scale, this husband-and-wife team were the behind-the-scenes tour de force of some of the biggest performers and well-known songs of the twentieth century. They wrote Aretha Franklin's "Cry Like a Baby," Ray Charles's "Let's Go Get Stoned," almost all of Marvin Gaye and Tammi Terrell's hits including a karaoke favorite "Ain't No Mountain High Enough," and all the songs on Diana Ross's 1970s albums including "Reach Out and Touch (Somebody's Hand)." Meanwhile, their song "Solid as Barack"—a rewriting of "Solid as a Rock"—was part of Obama's 2009 inauguration. If you've ever danced, you've probably pulsated to music that bears their names.

But in the eighties and nineties, for those in their circle, they were best known for their Fourth of July white parties at their sprawling home in Westport, Connecticut. They had tennis courts, swimming pools, and all sorts of food—soul food and vegetarian—for entertaining. Since they had properties on both the east and west sides of Manhattan, people could grab chartered transportation to the event from there. They kept the free transportation continuously running between their homes, to ensure that anyone who wanted to participate could.[3]

Val's motto was spot on. She would always say, "When you come to this party, everyone's a star." And it was true. Everyone was equal.

---

3. While not a lot has been written about these parties, Talley's "Down South" provides a glimpse into them.

They were showing their love and appreciation not only for their fans but for humankind. However, if you didn't wear white, you got turned away at the door. They expected you to follow the rules. One time, someone wore a baseball cap that wasn't the right color and Nick took it away and gave him a white one. Nick was dapper to the max, always impeccably dressed to make a statement. Yet, there was an incredibly free energy: no tension, no envy, no jealousy, no outdressing so-and-so with such-and-such. People could just be.

There was always plenty of entertainment, but the party really got started when Nick and Val performed, with several wardrobe changes, of course. They had a great routine and would constantly tease each other, a hallmark of their decades-long marriage. It was a joyous time in the summer and I waited for it all year, every year. While the food and entertainment were of the utmost quality, the highlight of the white party was the chance to meet and converse with incredible people, from the unknowns such as myself to people like Maya Angelou and Oprah Winfrey, who moved mountains.

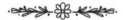

What these events articulated for me was the brilliance of Black women, pioneers in industries that did what they could to shut them out. Being in the presence of Black female excellence, really brought home the realization of how tenacious the people I met were in combatting the social structures that sought to keep them in their place. One of the people I crossed paths with was Barbara Harris, a behind-the-scenes juggernaut in the music industry. At the height of her musical career,

Barbara was a publicist and artist relations director during her time at Atlantic Records and a manager while at ABC Records. She worked with Roberta Flack years before I did, witnessing historic moments such as when Roberta sang for a fundraiser event at Bobby Kennedy's home in D.C., just months before his assassination. Barbara went on to lead the great Donny Hathaway's first promotional tour. What I admired most about her and why I considered her a mentor, was her ability as a Black woman to navigate the challenging waters of a very white and very male industry.

Barbara got her foot in the door by working at Queen Booking Agency, under Ruth Bowen—our country's first Black female booking agent. This agency, the brainchild of Dinah Washington, was run by Black people for Black people, in an era where white people pulled all the strings. Barbara worked with Aretha Franklin, Sammy Davis Jr., George Clinton, and numerous other legends. After about five years, a chance encounter with Henry Allen led to her moving to Atlantic Records and working with another impressive Black woman. Noreen Woods, who had become Vice President of Atlantic in 1974 after being hired almost two decades prior as a receptionist, was "the highest-ranking Black woman with a major record-company."[4]

However, moving from an all-Black company to a predominantly white one was a constant struggle. Barbara had to stand up for herself in the face of blatant disrespect. Her strategy was to dress well, not be a slouch, do her job flawlessly and not take anything from anybody. If she had to straighten men out, she would. If they made nasty jokes or

---

4. "Noreen Woods Appointed V.P. of Atlantic Records," *Jet Magazine*, December 26, 1974, p. 57.

touched her, she would take it to the streets. She was embodying the #metoo movement decades before it was trending. She didn't care if they called her a bitch. She did her job and did it well. From Atlantic, she moved to ABC, where she was made head of the New York office and was quite successful. But when the white guys in the office—mad at having a Black woman boss—succeeded in getting her removed, she ended up suing. She knew the risk of being blackballed by the industry, but it was her time to move on. She got into fashion, then art, then real estate while relishing it all. She would always tell me, "I'm in the business of working with beautiful things: clothes, people, art, music. Life is a challenge. I just roll with it." Barbara has been such an inspiration and a model for how to survive in the business.[5]

While Barbara supplied me the wisdom of succeeding in music, Oprah Winfrey and Maya Angelou bestowed the wisdom of thriving in life. Both were mainstays at the white parties, and throughout the years, as they both enjoyed a meteoric rise in their careers, they always remained consummate examples of humility and compassion.

Even though I have rubbed shoulders with some of the world's wealthiest or most famous people, I always approached these interactions as I would any other in my career. I would only do what needed to be done in my role as a member of a supporting team and was adamant at not confusing my personal life with my professional life. My contract, starting with Roberta Flack, stated that I didn't deal with pets, lovers, or homes. I didn't want to be responsible for anything that wasn't directly related to work. Distractions could affect my job performance and I took much pride in my work. This clinical approach to interacting

---

5. See Nathan's "Publicist Barbara Harris" for more information.

with famous people allowed me to do my job well, but also to avoid making a fool of myself like I did with John Lennon in the elevator. The white parties, however, by virtue of their very essence, made this clinical approach difficult to pull off because the whole point was to unwind and mingle.

At one particular party, I was minding my own business when I noticed out of the corner of my eye, Oprah and Maya sitting at a table nearby. They seemed to be trying to catch my attention, but I focused intently on the ground in front of me so that I wouldn't accidentally make eye contact. All of a sudden, a very flamboyant server tapped me on the shoulder and animatedly informed me that Maya and Oprah requested that I join their table.

I told him, "I can't, please. I can't. It's Maya and Oprah." My legs were shaking so much that the heels of my shoes began sinking into the grass, drilling the ground with nervous vibration.

Looking exacerbated, he retorted, "Girrrrl, stop being a drama queen and just go over there. I'm not going to tell them that their request has been denied. You don't do that to Oprah and Maya."

I sighed and followed him over.

As I sat down next to them, Maya told me in that soothing voice of hers, "I just wanted to tell you how lovely you look." I was rather taken aback and meekly thanked her for her kind words. Their warmth put me at ease right away. However, I was relieved when some other people started to come over so that the presence of these two queens could be shared amongst many people. I felt too small and too shy to take the brunt of their power alone. I could neither believe I had just met Maya and Oprah, nor could I get over how sweet they were.

Star struck wasn't the right word for the feelings swirling inside of me. I felt a profound connection to them because of some of the similarities in our upbringings—brutal beginnings that they were able to transform into lives that would touch millions of people. Whenever I would get down on myself or see no way out of a particular dark point, I would rely on their strength and tenacity. I let their words and performances help me find my path.

The three of us endured harrowing childhoods, although the effects on our lives manifested in different ways. Both Maya and Oprah were horrifically sexually abused at the age of eight and nine, respectively—the same age I began sleeping with a knife under my pillow. When Oprah told her family, they called her a liar.[6] When I told my mother about what was happening to my sister, she beat me. I spent much of my life wondering what would've happened if my mother had believed me. I thought that maybe she would've even been able to love me. But Maya's story allowed me to see the devastating toll of sexual abuse, even when family does believe you. When Maya's mother's boyfriend raped her, her family sought justice. But the justice system often fails girls and women. When her rapist only spent a day in jail even after receiving a guilty verdict, her uncles purportedly administered their own justice by murdering him.

Instead of her attacker's death freeing her, the violence—violence she had no control over but which was performed in her name—imprisoned her in a state of mutism for almost five years: "If I talked to anyone else that person might die too. Just my breath, carrying my words out, might poison people and they'd curl up and die...I had to stop talking." Those

---

6. For more information, see Garson's *Oprah Winfrey*.

words were so heavy for me. There were so many times in my childhood when I was rendered speechless, moments when I was forced to hold my tongue and when I didn't, I was punished. I remember devouring *I Know Why the Caged Bird Sings* because while our stories diverged in many ways, so much of what she said sounded like my life.[7]

In that book, Maya expressed many of the feelings that burdened me throughout my childhood. Through her years of writing, she eloquently showed how her spirit guided her and helped her find a way of freeing herself. Her words gifted her with peace, but they transformed so many more people than just herself. Her writings allowed me to finally not feel so alone. I was no longer the lone ranger. I now understood that I was part of an experience called life. This realization granted me freedom. Maya modeled how to make peace in a world teeming with violence and anger. Many people grow up with guidance from family, friends, the community, but I didn't have any of that, so I had to find another way to navigate life—through her wisdom and the wisdom of other strong women.

Those years of silence forced Maya to find solace in books, much like how the books I read opened worlds to me and dared me to dream of something different. I loved helping in the school library, the one space—other than my favorite climbing tree and Mama's house—that I really treasured from childhood. I was long out of school when I came across her books, but when I encountered them, I read each one voraciously. It was almost as if she was a fairy godmother, reaching into so many people with such beautiful hope and positivity. Until her, I always

---

7. Angelou, Maya. *I Know Why the Caged Bird Sings.* 1969, 1997. Caged Bird Legacy. Used by permission of Penguin Random House.

thought that there was nobody who looked like me, thought like me, felt like me. I finally learned it was okay to be me. Of all the people I consider messengers—put here on earth to advance humankind in some way—Maya Angelou was the most special to me. She made it clear to me why life was worth living, even if I would lose sight of this knowledge at points in my life.

The white parties allowed me to meet amazing people with diverse views on life. I never talked to a lot of people there, preferring to observe it all from a distance. These events were nothing but positive energy and an integral way for me to make human connections in my own way, which would help me through hard times.

Chapter 10: Getting Personal

Fig. 17. Mannequin wearing a Fabrice Simon dress in Alvenia's entryway. By Maya Angela Smith.

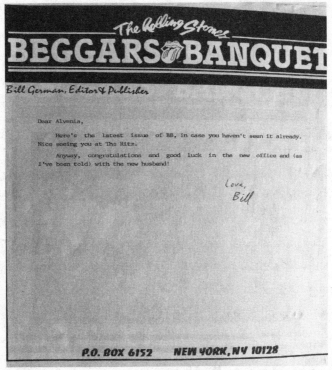

Fig. 18. Personal note from Bill German. By Maya Angela Smith.

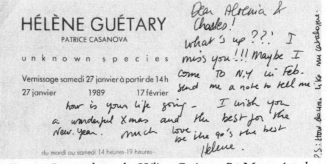

Fig. 19. Personal note by Hélène Guétary. By Maya Angela Smith.

When you step inside Alvenia's apartment, you are immediately greet-ed by a mannequin dressed to the nines with matching shoes resting against its base (Fig. 17). This mannequin goes through a series of wardrobe changes each season, but the strand of pearls always remains the same. This mannequin signals to the casual observer that the occupants of this apartment have exquisite taste. It's not until you get to know Alvenia that you realize that she is doing more than simply displaying high fashion as a way of cueing any visitors to her sartorial sensibilities. Alvenia sees this exhibit as a means of paying homage to her favorite designer, Fabrice Simon, who outfitted her for practically every glitzy event that she attended during her years in fashion and music. When he succumbed to AIDS at the young age of forty-seven in 1998, Alvenia was devastated and decided that his memory would live on in the one place that she had control over, her home.[1]

The glamorous entrance to Alvenia's home also belies the financial issues that Alvenia has shouldered since getting out of the music business. Her large treasure trove of Fabrice dresses has often been one of her only forms of currency when she finds herself in dire straits. Because she doesn't like the feeling of owing anyone, she has been known to gift dresses to thank people for helping her through hard times. However, she doesn't part with these dresses lightly. They are the last tangible reminder of her decades-long friendship with Fabrice.

The mannequin signals a key part of Alvenia's life, but does not convey the true depth of her story until Alvenia decides to share her story on her

---

1. For more information, see Schiro's "Fabrice Simon."

terms. If you really want to know the essence of who she is, you must work to get to know her because the clues she leaves are only a small part of her narrative. Through our friendship and our partnership on this book, I have gained access to large swaths of her life to the point where I think I truly know her, but it seems like each day something new unfolds. Imagine my surprise that it took a few years into our relationship to learn Alvenia was married. It was only then that she showed me evidence of this part of her life.

Hidden in stacks of papers, spirited away in dark recesses of her home, these reminders seldom emerge. They provide a stark contrast to the memorabilia from her illustrious career that she proudly displays on her walls. One clue of this cloistered part of her story is this short note (Fig. 18) from Bill German, editor of the Rolling Stones Beggars Banquet *magazine and author of the memoir* Under their Thumb, *which chronicles his life on the road with the Stones. Bill had included a personal note in an issue of his magazine in which he mentioned Alvenia's new husband. That was the first I had heard of said husband. Another marker of this mysterious life event is a note that her friend, artist Hélène Guétary, had sent Alvenia, along with an invitation to her art opening in Paris (Fig. 19).[2] The note was addressed to both Alvenia and Charles. The mystery husband finally had a name. In bringing her romantic life to the surface, Alvenia was finally ready to place this missing puzzle piece into the story she had crafted for me.*

When people learn about the topsy-turvy, wild ride my life has been and they think about my career choices—both as a model, where I was

---

2. For more information on Guétary, see her website at https://www.heleneguetary.com/.

constantly the center of male attention and as a female publicist in the male-dominated world of rock and roll—they assume that my existence was fueled by sex and drugs. Couple that with the promiscuity that our society lazily attaches to Black women, most people were unable to see me for anything other than a sexual object when I was in my prime. While there is nothing wrong with sexuality and being free to love and lust after whomever you want, that wasn't the type of freedom I cared about. The only freedom I sought in my life was to escape Kansas—and its memories of the boy who threw the Coke bottle, the shop owner who spat at me to get out of his store, and the policeman who pinned me down—and to explore a world that was far, far away from that dismal place. In this world I sought, I could make myself anew and shine at anything I put my mind to.

But just because I left Kansas didn't mean I left the close-minded mentality that marred my childhood. As I worked to create my narrative, the world around me insisted on writing its own story about me and did so in a wholly inauthentic way. While I saw myself as a person, people often reduced me to my race and my gender and the intersections of the two. Nothing made this clearer than when I moved into my apartment on 58th street.

I started looking for an apartment in New York, while I was on the road with the Stones in the early eighties. I was based in Paris during their European Tour, enjoying the lifestyle but compelled to set down firmer roots in the Big Apple. I pretty much told everyone who would listen that I was on the hunt for an apartment, preferably on the Upper West Side. When a friend called me excitedly with the promise of my dream apartment, I squealed, "Take it, take it, take it!" She had found a place a block away from Columbus Circle, just south of Central Park. I contacted the Stones office and instructed Debbie, the right-hand to the accountant, to put down six months' rent in advance. I wasn't going to let anything stand in the way of me and my ability to create a New York home.

A few weeks later, I returned from Europe and moved into my new apartment. Hector, the maintenance man, was one of the first people I met and the only person of color I ever saw in my new building. He was a hardworking fellow who was attentive to the needs of the building, as if it were his own home. I asked him to find out how many people lived in the building. I then bought packages of fancy chocolate, attached a brief note to each one and left this gift at each of my neighbor's doors as a way of introducing myself. But when I was in the elevator or entering the building, no one I ran into would speak to me. It was bizarre. Granted, this was New York, but New Yorkers reserve their gruff manner for people on the street, not for neighbors they see in their building on a daily basis. Based on life experiences, I figured that they treated me like this because I was the only Black person in the building. I didn't tell my friend who had found the place, because I didn't want to talk about racial issues with her and I didn't want her to feel bad for finding a place where people treated me with such contempt. In fact, there was no one I could talk to. I was surrounded by white people who wouldn't understand. So, I would often go to the park and talk to the trees.

One day, I went on a walk with Hector and I asked him to be honest with me. I really wanted to know why I was getting such cold treatment from everyone. Hector looked down at his feet. He always had such kind eyes, but I could tell he diverted his glance to hide a sense of shame. He finally confided in me, "Alvenia, they think you're a lady of the night."

"A what?"

"A lady of the night," he repeated.

At that moment I nearly fell over. While I had assumed that my neighbors' treatment of me was based on my race, I never could've imagined the depravity of their thinking. What was a lady of the night doing wearing designer clothes and putting down six months' rent at a time? How did they all afford to live in the building? Whatever careers they had, couldn't I have them, too? I felt the urge to get angry, but I reminded myself that anger never got me anything good in this world. When the fury dissipated, all I felt was emptiness. I told myself that I would let them have their fantasy. Racism wasn't my problem, it was theirs. They had no idea what I had gone through as a child, what racist vitriol I had endured. There was no way I was going to let them take away my joy—my joy of home, my joy of life, my joy of being. I decided at that moment that I would kill them with kindness, not because I wanted them to be happy but because that was the only way I knew how to survive. When I let their hate and ignorance eat me up, I was only harming myself. Ignorance was everywhere. If I was going to navigate an ignorant world, I needed to do so with my sanity as my top priority.

One day, Mick said he wanted to come by and check out my place. You should've seen my neighbors' reactions when they realized who he was and so by association, who I was. Their whole demeanor toward me changed. They showed me basic civility by greeting me in the hallway. They smiled when I walked by. I didn't care that I could taste the saccharin dripping from their breath. Again, it wasn't my problem. It was theirs. When they wanted tickets to something, I would supply them. Tickets, autographed pictures, anything. Mick knew what I was up to and made sure I had whatever I needed. We never really talked in depth about race, but he acknowledged it existed. At every Stones concert, he would hold up his fingers and wink at me. The number of fingers corresponded with the number of Black people he saw in the crowd. It was our inside joke.

In some regards, it may look as if I was buying my neighbors' respect, but I didn't see it that way. I had resolved long ago to see everyone for their humanity, even though I knew most people were oblivious of mine. Treating people how I deserved to be treated was my way of being human, not for them, but for myself.

Despite the reception of my neighbors, I loved living in my apartment. I finally felt grounded after so much time on the road. It was nice to focus on me and my personal life instead of constantly tending to the needs of others. One evening, soon after moving in, I was invited to a party by the Bismarck brothers at Sutton Place. The apartment opened onto a deck that overlooked Roosevelt Island. The view was great, but the company was utterly boring. It was one of those snooty, stiff parties with no music, where everyone was engaged in name-dropping and showing off their fancy clothes. I was entrenched in the world of rock, so I could name-drop with the best of them, but it seemed like vapid and idle chit chat. After about half an hour I snuck out so that I could go dancing downtown on Varrick and Vandam. As I slipped into the elevator, a dashing man followed me. He started going on and on about how tedious that whole event was, and we had a good laugh. I told him I was headed to Soho for some real entertainment. He introduced himself as Gerald Parkes and then shyly asked if he could join me. There was something intriguing about him so I told him he could tag along.

We needed to stop by my place first so I could change clothes. There was no way I was going to my favorite dancing spot looking like some stuck-up yuppie. I was a chameleon that way and could move in many different crowds. I apologized as I showed Gerald my apartment, which lacked furniture. I had just gotten off the road. At the same time, I was so proud to show off my place, my first real grown-up apartment. It was a far cry from those years of sharing fifth-floor walkups with spotty heating such as when I lived with Jerry Hall or Johnny McLaughlin. My days of being a starving artist were over.

As we pulled up to the club, I warned my impromptu date of how much I loved to dance, "If you don't feel like dancing, don't worry. You can hold the table while I dance."

He chuckled, but I don't think he was ready for how long I was out there. I danced. And danced. And danced. He joined me for some of it—he was actually a better dancer than he looked like he'd be—and then spent the rest of the time smiling at me while I did my thing. He dropped me off at two a.m., kissing my hand like a perfect gentleman, then he asked if I would like to accompany him back to Soho the following day to see the galleries. I was enjoying this ride and accepted his offer.

We were pretty much inseparable for the next few weeks—relishing a mix of highbrow and lowbrow entertainment. He would whisk me away to fancy restaurants after afternoons of looking at exquisite art in the finest museums and then we would change directions and hit all the comedy hot spots. The most memorable experience was Whoopi Goldberg's comedic debut off Broadway in 1983. She had the audience in stitches at her one-woman show, going between different characters with impressive ease. I was particularly bowled over by her valley girl impression. I had spent enough years in Los Angeles to know that she nailed it. I remember feeling overwhelming pride that this woman with rich, dark skin and powerful locs was commanding the attention of everyone in a field where people like her were written one-dimensionally, if written about at all. I realized her act had so many dimensions because she wrote her material herself.

Gerald opened this whole, new, interesting world to me to the point where he became my world and I was loving every minute I spent with him. We started off as friends. I never once even thought about dating until one evening he leaned over after a particularly exceptional date and kissed me. I was taken aback by it, not because I didn't want to date him but because I didn't know what to do. He was so nice, so sweet and patient, but we weren't intimate for a while because I was confused. It was through him that I learned intimacy, because I finally believed someone loved me. I finally *allowed* someone to love me. While others around me created fantasies about my being some loose, roving sexpot, such as the neighbors in my building who labeled me "a lady of the night" simply for being a Black woman with money, I had spent the first four decades of my life just trying to understand what love was and what it could be.

Our relationship continued to blossom. He bought a townhouse on 76th and Central Park West because of me and I began living between my place and there. He also had his other home on 82nd street, not far from Mick's. He bought and sold big businesses for a living. He was a serious money mover and provided us with anything we could ever want. Yet, he wouldn't make a decision without us agreeing on things together. We decorated the townhome the way I wanted. We had a great garden that reminded me of my childhood farm. We traveled the world, from tropical islands like the Bahamas and Jamaica, to his hometown in England. On that trip to England, I met his entire family, not even putting it together at the time that he was thinking of proposing at some point soon.

This period of my life seemed like a dream when I reflect back on it. Sometimes I wonder if it actually happened, but just like with any dream, reality has to set in some time. One night, a couple years into our relationship, I was sound asleep in the loft while Gerald was traveling on one of his frequent business trips. I bolted upright after I dreamed that I saw him as clear as day in bed with a brunette. I was panting to the point of almost hyperventilating. This dream of Gerald cheating on me seemed so real, but how could it be? I just chalked it up as jealousy because women were constantly trying to get close to him. I took slow, deep breaths and willed myself to sleep, spending the rest of the night approximating slumber but never quite succeeding.

The next day, I prepared for a dinner party that we were going to throw for some of our friends. I was a killer cook and glad to have something to keep my mind off the nagging premonition. Early in the afternoon, his secretary called to say that plans had changed and that it would just be the two of us. I kept praying that my dream wasn't true and functioned on autopilot. I prepared a less lavish dinner than planned and then set out rose petals from the door to the bedroom—something I always did when he returned from a business trip. Once I finally learned to love, I did so fully.

He entered the apartment with his suitcase. When I greeted him at the door, he was putting on a brave face, but there was a slight twitch in the corner of his mouth that alerted me to hidden emotions. I took another deep breath. He went into the bathroom to freshen up and I clutched the back of the chair to steady myself until he joined me at the dinner table. As we sat down for dinner, I couldn't take it any longer.

Before I could think through my words, I blurted, "She's a brunette, isn't she?"

He looked at me, stunned. How could I have known? He tried to grab my hand, but I snatched it away as he pleaded that it was just a one-night stand. At that moment, something snapped and I lost touch with all reality.

I took a walking stick—I collected them from my travels—and started thrashing about, destroying all the art hanging on the walls and adorning the tables. When I realized the level of my destruction, I ran out of our home and caught a cab to my apartment. When I flashed through the building, I told the doorman not to let Gerald in. I then hid out in my apartment for days and refused calls from everyone.

When my heart broke, it took my mind with it. I never knew what it was like to set myself up for betrayal because I had never allowed myself to love in this way before. Now that I had, it was the worst feeling in the world. I didn't have any friends to go to, at least none with whom I wanted to talk about this. I knew lots of people and hung out with them, but they didn't really know me. Once again, I was alone.

In some ways, I wish my story ended there, in a ball of flames, because at least my destruction would've been spectacular and final. Instead, I drew out my destruction with a slow burn by inexplicably turning toward the first man I saw and marrying him.

Charles had been lusting after me for a long time. A Swiss man born in Kenya, he had met me through our mutual friends, Julio Mario Santo Domingo and Vera Rechulski, who I knew from my time in Switzerland. While I was with Gerald, all my Swiss friends were converging on New York City. They were from powerful and wealthy families that had multiple homes throughout the world. Anyone who was anyone owned property in New York. When Charles moved to New York City and connected with these friends, he started hovering around me. Because of Gerald's infidelity, I was neither in a good place nor capable of making the best decisions. With Charles sort of floating around in the background, I decided to glom onto him for no reason. I somehow reasoned he would take the pain away, perhaps like a parasite that numbs its host before extracting blood.

Charles contacted me when I was spiraling out of control and I decided then and there that I would marry him. There had never been any attraction between us, at least not on my end and through our whole time together, there was no romance. Pretty much in no time we were married. I don't even know how it happened. There are pictures of my bridal shower that Roberta Flack threw for me at her house, but I don't really remember being there. I don't know why no one thought to caution me about what I was doing. Maybe they did and I just didn't listen. That whole sequence of my life was like a waking dream.

By 1986 I was married. I remember nothing of the wedding ceremony. I couldn't say what my dress looked like. All I know is that on my wedding night we exchanged not even a kiss. He simply fell asleep, while I was lying catatonic next to him. I should have gotten up the next day and asked for an annulment, but I was full of pride. It was absolutely insane what I did to myself. Nobody knew, but I just destroyed myself.

And destruction felt so good. I saw myself as a failure that needed to be eradicated. It's still so hard to believe that I let this betrayal destroy me. My core being was shattered from places that I did not know existed inside me. I always thought I loved myself, but I realized that at that moment, I didn't really.

My bad decisions didn't end with the act of getting married. I was foolish enough to have Charles take control of my finances. Here I was, this strong, powerful woman who was doing well financially and I just gave over the reins to Charles. I reasoned that because he had graduated from some famous school for finance, he could do a better job with my money than I could. He seemed to have a successful business and I just didn't pay attention. I had checked out completely. I threw all my energy back into my work, but that was also not bringing me any joy. Then my dear Antonio Lopez died in 1987, so my world continued to crumble down around me, even when I thought there were no bricks left to fall.

The most shocking thing is that I somehow regained some normalcy—not healthy normalcy molded out of learned lessons and finding peace, but the type of imitation normalcy that comes from pretending everything is okay. Even though there was nothing marital between Charles and me, I did things like get Swiss citizenship and procure a Swiss passport. I acted like this thing called a marriage, was actually a marriage—instead of the biggest mistake of my life. But the façade could only go on for so long. I wanted him away from me, so eventually, I asked him to leave. I think he moved back to Switzerland.

On paper, somehow, we are still married. We never officially got a divorce and since our joint account no longer exists, the money I had put in it is gone forever. I still beat myself up for not being smarter about my love life and my finances. I attribute these bad decisions to growing up with no guidance. But on days when I see clearly, I recognize that my actions stemmed from never really dealing with the pain life has thrown my way, instead, thinking that escaping my troubles was the only way that I could move forward. While my reaction to Gerald's betrayal started my spin out of control, the death of Bill Graham five years later knocked me completely out of orbit.

Chapter 11: Finding Solid Ground

BILL GRAHAM PRESENTS

March 17, 1989

TO WHOM IT MAY CONCERN:

I have been professionally acquainted with Ms. Alvenia Bridges since 1981, when we had occasion to work together on the Rolling Stones U.S. tour; I as tour director and she as publicity representative for the group. Subsequent to that tour, we worked together on the Rolling Stones 1982 tour of Europe; Live Aid in 1985; Amnesty International's U.S. tour in 1986; and the Soviet-American Peace Concert in Moscow in 1987, among other projects.

At all times, Alvenia has handled her press and publicity responsibilities in a most efficient and professional manner. However, I believe her true talent lies in the manner in which she relates to the people she comes into contact with in the course of her work. Regardless of one's social or professional status - be it artist, industry executive, journalist, office worker or concert patron - Alvenia's personal warmth and professional attitude are always in synch with the needs of the occasion. In the entertainment industry, with its inherent emotionalism and egos, Alvenia's attributes as a "people person" are most beneficial and, at times, vital. Her affirmative attitude and sensitivity to others, combined with her professional skills and experience, make her a most capable and rather unique individual who would be a positive addition to any production team.

I recommend Alvenia Bridges for any job which she feels capable of handling.

Cheers!

Bill Graham

Bill Graham

BG:jan

P.O. Box 1994, San Francisco, CA 94101   415/541-0800

Fig. 20. Recommendation letter by Bill Graham. By Maya Angela Smith.

Fig. 21. Poster of memorial concert for Bill Graham, Steve Kahn, and Melissa Gold. By Maya Angela Smith.

Alvenia told me about how one day a few years ago she found a letter from Bill dated March 17, 1989, that she had tucked away (Fig. 20). It had been years since she laid eyes on it and had only found it because she was trying to compile information for the memoir. When she proudly showed me the piece of paper, I was surprised that it was a letter of recommendation addressed in the formal and sterile convention of "to whom it may concern." The way she had described it, I had imagined that it was some secret love note that only she and Bill knew about, not some document that could be used to seek future employment. But the effect that this find had on Alvenia was magical. She made it a habit to read his words every morning as part of her daily ritual. I asked Alvenia why this letter meant so much to her and she replied that it had come out of nowhere when she first received it. She had never asked for a letter of recommendation. Bill had taken it upon himself to write one. For her, it was tangible proof of just how much he respected her. She then handed over the letter so I could read it in its entirety.

The beginning of the letter was what I would expect of something of this genre. It detailed how Bill knew Alvenia and projects that they had worked on together. However, when I started reading the second paragraph, I began to understand just how special this letter was. Bill had taken what many perceive as a genre void of emotion and imbued it with incredibly touching language, while still adhering to the expected norms of recommendation letters. I knew what Alvenia thought of her abilities in the music industry. To see how her closest colleague saw her granted me a whole other perspective. Bill's description of Alvenia was almost poetic and undoubtedly conveyed just how much she meant to him:

"Regardless of one's social or professional status—be it artist, industry executive, journalist, office worker or concert patron—Alvenia's personal warmth and professional attitude are always in synch with the needs of the occasion. In the entertainment industry, with its inherent emotionalism and egos, Alvenia's attributes as a 'people person' are most beneficial and, at times, vital. Her affirmative attitude and sensitivity to others, combined with her professional skills and experience, make her a most capable and

rather unique individual who would be a positive addition to any production team."

The poster of Bill Graham (Fig. 21) hangs prominently in Alvenia's kitchen. Lipstick residue is smudged on his face. I learned early on that Alvenia dutifully kisses his image each morning—a gesture at the center of her morning ritual. She would also sometimes talk to his poster and ask for guidance when she had to make a difficult decision. He is one of several important people enshrined on Alvenia's breakfast-nook altar who gets a dose of Alvenia's daily love. But he is by far the one she lingers over the longest. Before she told me their story, I wondered what this guy meant to her. Between the frantic way that he entered Alvenia's life and the violent way that he departed from it, each kiss is imbued with the urgency and love of someone who has not quite let go. Each morning, it's as if Alvenia leaves this offering in hopes that he will not only be granted safe passage to whatever comes next, but that she will one day be fully able to accept that he is no longer physically in her life.

While my personal life was in shambles and I was falling back on my old patterns of avoidance instead of dealing with my issues, I resolved to at least make my career have some meaning. Before my breakdown, I was usually game for tackling whatever Bill Graham threw my way, but in light of these recent personal developments, I threw myself into my work with almost reckless abandon. I just kept going and going, always looking for an excuse not to slow down and take stock of my life. At that moment I thought I could shine by becoming a more integral part of Bill Graham Presents.

One day in 1991, Bill called me and said, "Alvenia, I understand your dream. The next time you're in San Francisco, I would love to get dinner with you and discuss the possibilities." I was ecstatic. I had seen how good Bill was at making dreams a reality with his tenacity and unwavering support. While he could be brutal to people in the name of getting his way, he had an unflinching loyalty to those he championed. I was going to be in California the last Friday in October and gleefully marked it on my calendar.

At some point, plans changed. Huey Lewis and the News, who were playing at Concord Pavilion, ended up adding an extra show when their first one sold out so quickly. Bill explained to me that he wanted to be at the concert as a show of appreciation and asked for us to take a raincheck on our dinner. I recall being irrationally upset. Bill had a million projects going on, so it was completely reasonable for him to have to make choices when things popped up, but I hated how this decision negatively impacted me. I was so convinced that a new career opportunity was the only way I was going to move past all the questionable decisions I'd made in the last five years, that I had to work hard not to resent anyone or anything that stood in the way.

Bill and his girlfriend Melissa Gold lived in Marin County, north of San Francisco. Since the recent Loma Prieta earthquake had made Bay Area traffic even worse than normal, especially with the closure of the damaged Bay Bridge, Bill's preferred mode of transportation quickly became his private helicopter, piloted by his friend Steve "Killer" Kahn. I learned years later that their ride to the Concord Pavilion on the night of Friday, October 25, 1991, had been anxiety-inducing. Chatting with people backstage, both Bill and Melissa described the harrowing take-off on their way to the concert after a major storm had turned a warm, sunny day into a cold, menacing night. Numerous people at the reception had offered ideas on how the trio could avoid flying in the storm for their return home, whether by staying overnight in Concord or by being driven home instead.

Various reports noted that while the Oakland Flight Service Station had recommended that they not take the helicopter because of limited visibility and inclement weather, Bill, Melissa, and Steve took an opportunity to make their move when the rains let up for a bit. As soon as they were in the air, the rains kicked up again with a violent fervor. Ravaging winds carried sheets of water horizontally, crashing into the helicopter, and as Steve fought to maintain control, the helicopter was flung into a transmission tower and exploded on impact.

I first found out about Bill's death the following morning when Alan Dunn, Mick's right-hand man, called me. "Did you hear about Bill?" he asked cautiously. Having spent the night moping around in my apartment, I had not turned on the news and had no idea what he was talking about. As he laid out the little information he had, my knees started to buckle. I sat down on the floor of my apartment, needing to feel solid ground below me. I had ended up not going to California that weekend, still upset by our cancelled meeting. Now I would never have the chance to see him again.

When I called Jan Simmons, she solemnly told me, "Bill's not here." She must've noted the tinge of frantic despair in my voice because she added, "You're not well." I knew that as much as I wanted to get to San Francisco, it wouldn't bring Bill back. I decided not to attend the funeral, or the memorial concert staged in Golden Gate Park the week after Bill's death. I read how 300,000 people paid their respects to Bill, Steve, and Melissa as they listened to Santana, the Grateful Dead and several other of Bill's former acts eulogize the man that helped to make them who they were. [1]

I started to nonsensically wonder if I had caused his death. The moment Bill called off our meeting, I cocooned myself with negative energy driven by my lack of patience. Bill hadn't said he wouldn't go through with supporting my career ambitions, he just wasn't available to meet on that one day. Yet, I wasn't thinking straight and imagined that I had somehow inadvertently willed his demise. It took months to convince myself how silly I was being and as I finally let go of the supernatural story that I was telling myself, the utter grief of realizing one of my closest friends was dead fully sank in.

I would replay my fondest memories of Bill in my head. The one I kept watching on repeat the most, was when we went to a party that Bill threw for Tito Puente's birthday at the top of the Twin Towers. Celia Cruz showed up as a surprise guest and took control of the party with her booming voice. When Bill took me on the dance floor and twirled me around, I felt my heart fly in sync with the fringe of my Fabrice dress. Bill had his salsa moves down. I also thought about the encouraging recommendation letter he had written me without my asking. I would read it over and over again to help me fall asleep. While it hadn't been obvious until then, Bill had transformed from that gruff man who yelled at me when I first showed up at his office a decade earlier to the most important person in my life, my hero.

I went underground for three months as I grieved and tried to sort out my thoughts. No one could come near me. I thought my world was

---

1. For more information, see Lambert's "Bill Graham" and Weber's "Bay Area Plays Tribute to Graham."

over. I had been slowly dwindling into a former shell of myself for the past half-decade as I weathered failed romance and heartbreak, and Bill's passing extinguished what tiny bit of my soul I had managed to preserve.

Bill's death precipitated my exit from the industry. My heart was just no longer in it. I would help with events here and there and I would occasionally think about getting back into the business such as when Patti Labelle approached me, but in the end, I realized that era of my life was over. I had made major career changes before. I figured I could do so again. I started applying for sales associate positions in high-end department stores such as Chanel and Bergdorf's. I knew a lot about fashion and even more about thriving in high pressure environments. I was convinced my skills were transferrable. Each place I went, they told me I was overdressed. How could I be overdressed? These were snooty, high-end stores. I realized that they were trying to say that I didn't fit in with their clientele without spelling out why I didn't fit in. By this point, I had no more fight in me. I let insecurity get the best of me and my ambition slowly wasted away.

Without a career and without savings to cushion my fall as I spiraled into depression, I had to alter the way I lived. I started renting out rooms in the apartment, eventually exchanging my own room for a couch in the living room. Some of my living situations were great, others were disillusioning. There were those who treated me like the maid and others who straight up stole from me. For instance, when I went to the hospital for a routine procedure, two roommates stole rent money, furniture, and precious memorabilia before skipping town. It seemed like one thing after another further unraveled my life. I was losing what little I had left.

It took a serious illness for me to wrest my future from complete implosion. While I was in the hospital for a sudden major life-threatening issue, I had a visitor. Something spiritual. More a presence than an image who let me know that it just wasn't my time. In an encouraging way, it said something like "Let's go. What are you doing here?" At that moment I began to physically heal so fast that the doctors were amazed. But my ailments were not just physical. The Spirit showed me that there was a lot I had to do inside myself to figure out how I got here. I needed to understand how I had allowed the world to take away my self-esteem, my courage, my chutzpah, everything I have, me. I had been reduced to a skeleton. I had convinced myself that I had nothing left to give. The Spirit reminded me that I needed to get back to being a fighter, the girl who took on the Ku Klux Klan. The woman who held her own in a world dominated by men. I had turned myself into what I wanted to be many times before. I could do it again.

But to really get back to being myself, I ironically needed to change. I realized that everything in this world that allowed me to survive, and even thrive at times, was no longer effective. I had spent my whole adult life filling every moment with plans and activities so that I wouldn't have to deal with the foundational issues of who I was and what my purpose on this planet was. Everything I had done since my escape from Kansas was connected to convincing the world that I could succeed even when it expected failure. But my way of succeeding in the world revolved around ignoring how the world actually worked.

For instance, when I was huddled up in my favorite tree asking God to relieve me of all racial karma after my failed attempt at integrating that school, I thought I had found the answer to my societal problems. Through this colorblind approach, I was going to rise above the turmoil, ignore its stinging blows, and just grit my teeth. But that tactic wasn't sustainable because each time I swallowed an injustice or smiled in the face of ignorance, I was letting the root cause fester and passing the hard work on to somebody else. I was also compromising my well-being to avoid confrontation. But, willing the world to be colorblind did not make it so. Challenging people to see the world for what it was, instead of what we wished it to be was much more difficult but more authentic. I could no longer just ignore. I had to actively resist but do so without sacrificing my soul. In questions of race, I'm still finding my voice.

Similarly, when I left Kansas, ridding myself of that pathetic excuse for a stepfather, I patted myself on the back. I had kept my promise to my grandmother and was rewarded in kind. I did what needed because if I had stayed, I was prepared to go to the dark side: death and jail were the only futures I saw. But while I avoided this fate, my sister had to shoulder the full burden. It wasn't until years later that I learned that Ed Madden had threatened to kill our mother if my sister did not give herself up to him every Saturday night. While I was exploring the world, she was securing our mother's safety one violation at a time.

If I was to move forward and truly heal, I needed to reconnect with my family. This required me to forgive myself for the guilt I still harbored for leaving them in harm's way and to forgive those who had done the harming. I thought leaving Kansas was going to be tough but letting all the associations I had with Kansas back in—even if I had no intention of ever setting foot there again—was going to be one of the biggest challenges of my life.

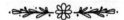

In order to get myself back on track, I went to my neighborhood branch of the New York Public Library—just like when I was a kid and would go to the school library—and I looked for guidance among the musty treasure trove of books. I thought about visiting the self-help section but then felt compelled to seek out Maya Angelou's wisdom. I first picked up *I Know Why the Caged Bird Sings*, reunited with the first book in my life that let me know that I was not alone. It was what I needed all those years ago but not this time. I then moved to *Mom & Me & Mom*, her most recent book, which she wrote to work through her resentment towards her mother. The premise resonated fully with me, but even this wasn't what unlocked my heart. Instead, it was a passage at the beginning of *Letter to My Daughter* that finally presented the balm I yearned for: "I have made many mistakes and no doubt will make more before I die. When I have seen pain, when I have found that my ineptness has caused displeasure, I have learned to accept my responsibility and to forgive myself first, then to apologize to anyone injured by my misreckoning...You may not control all the events that happen to you, but you can decide not to be reduced by them. Try to be a rainbow in someone's cloud."[2]

---

2. Angelou, Maya. *Letter to my Daughters.* 2008. Caged Bird Legacy. Used by permission of Penguin Random House.

She was giving me permission to forgive myself, because ultimately, if I was going to move forward, I had to love myself unconditionally. Daily affirmations of love for myself continue even until this day—ignited by Maya Angelou's words of gentle urging. However, this book did even more, because it forced me to imagine myself from a different perspective. Since the words were coming from a mother figure, they called on me to visualize my mother asking forgiveness of herself and then of me. Zonnetta died before she ever got that chance, but I could finally allow myself to envision a world where she did want to apologize. And, perhaps, just perhaps, I saw glimpses of an apology forming and hadn't even realized it. It flashed on me: the only piece of mail that she ever sent me was to inform me of Ed Madden's death. I didn't know what to make of the contents of that envelope when it first arrived. There was nothing inside but a newspaper clipping of Ed Madden's obituary. But at the insistence of Maya Angelou's words, I started to believe that this was her manner of apologizing the only way she knew how.

My body exhaled involuntarily as I made this realization at my table amongst the book stacks. I had spent all my life wondering why Zonnetta didn't love me, not considering that maybe she just didn't know how. She was navigating an abusive world as well. In ignoring the pain that she caused people by her words, her actions, and her inactions, she found her own way of escape. While running away from family and Jim Crow was how I survived, she chose denial and apathy to dress her wounds. While I will never condone what she let happen to her children, the only way that I can start to repair my soul is to forgive her, not just on my behalf but on hers. In the end, I am grateful to her. She was a carrier to get me here. She may not have provided the loving home I craved or the guidance I sought, but she brought me into the world. Even though I was currently wallowing in my deepest despair, I could look back on my life and admire what I achieved while still cognizant of what was left for me to do.

As I was slowly opening up myself for family, my siblings must have felt a pull to reunite as well because they entered my life in surprising ways. Robert tracked me down, probably through Cousin Larry, and opened his arms wide as he welcomed me back into his life. While we never met up in person before he passed away in 2010, he sent me a copy of his book *I Beat Dyslexia: So Can You*, which he published years after working with children in his community in Washington State to overcome their academic difficulties stemming from learning differences. Somehow, he didn't allow all the unkind words he endured as a kid to demoralize him. He was able to overcome others' ignorance and spite, as well as his learning disorder, and with this freedom he dedicated his life to making sure others would never feel the way he did as a child. He lived in the same hell I had and was still able to love himself, his family, and me.

I had felt like I let my brother down for all those years, but through his gesture of finding me, I realized that I was holding on to guilt that he had let go of long ago. Robert and I had always been close. If anyone was going to reconcile with me, it would be Robert. But could my sweet sister forgive me for abandoning her?

When I escaped, I left her in the care of that man—that monster who scraped away a little bit of her humanity every Saturday night. It took me decades to find permission to forgive myself for not only leaving her but for refusing to speak with any of my immediate family for years. When I cut ties with Kansas, I left that world completely. When people asked me where my family was, I said I didn't have one. I wasn't ready to deal with them. What must my rupture with the family have been like for my sister, who did nothing to deserve that?

But she had been doing the work that I had avoided all those years as I ran from city to city and career to career, because when we reconnected, she had nothing but forgiveness for me. Whatever strength that she was born with, that allowed her to pay for our mother's survival with her own flesh was the same strength that fed her endless fount of forgiveness. She had forgiven me. She had forgiven our mother. She had forgiven everyone that allowed these weekly visits to happen. But most of all, she had forgiven Ed Madden.

As my sister became a staple in my life again, I began to piece together all those years of absence. I learned about her life and the journey she had to take to arrive at a place of forgiveness. While it is not my place to tell all the details of her story, it's important to know that she had her own experience with rock bottom. One day when she was sitting at a stoplight, she decided it was time to make own escape: she would hit the accelerator and let the cross traffic take her away. Just as she was about to step on the gas, God visited her and told her plainly but with compassion, "I'm not ready for you, but you will be okay." That was the moment that changed her life. She has since relied on her church community to help guide her through all of life's struggles, consoled by this offer of light amidst so much darkness.

While I also believe in a higher power, my spirituality has taken a different path. I like to say that I'm non-denominational with God and Jesus on the side. The church of my childhood was not what guided me. I associated it with yet another place where I didn't really belong. I would get in trouble because I would become so moved by the music that I would clap my hands or tap my feet. For some reason, these displays were forbidden and so I realized that the way I wanted to worship was not the way that others expected me to. But my first recollection of the Spirit—and I'm not sure when I started calling it "the Spirit"—was through my grandmother. When Mama said, "Finish high school and I'll get you out," I had an overwhelming comprehension that the Spirit was speaking through her. When I looked at her, I only saw light and that light guided me to figure out what I could and should do in order to make her promise come true.

Perhaps this is why I have always been drawn to gothic structures. No matter where I was in the world, whether deejaying in Portofino or putting on rock concerts in the largest cities on the planet, I made it a habit of visiting gothic cathedrals. There was something about their monumental stature and immense darkness pierced by light filtered through ornate stained-glass windows that drew me to these spaces. The light that overpowered this seemingly monumental darkness perfectly represented what the Spirit meant to me and the silence that reverberated within its walls was so conducive to meditation and prayer, that I could finally let my mind relax.

It was in a moment of meditation that I realized that I was born with the Spirit. It was in there, waiting to be brought forth. I just needed someone like my grandmother to tap into it. I reasoned that while sometimes the Spirit would show up as a little voice in my head, other times it would present itself through the people I come in contact with—people like John Von Neumann, or James Finney, or Maya Angelou, or Bill Graham, or so many other important people in my life. They have always guided me when I needed the push. However, while all these years I thanked these chance encounters for laying out my path in life, a path I hoped would take me far, far away from Kansas, it was actually family—my grandmother—that provided that original beacon of light.

By reconnecting with my sister and brother, I became reacquainted with the importance of family. Through them, I also met all the other siblings I never got a chance to know because of how I left Kansas without looking back. They told me of the wonderful things Zonnetta had done for them in her life. They had a very different image of her than I did, which made me realize how much she had changed. I will never know if my leaving was the catalyst that she needed to approach her family differently. All I do know, is how grateful I am that they got to experience the best of her, the parts of her I only saw glimpses of when I was a kid. While I lived my dream of traveling the world—visiting the places that I had first encountered on my globe and talking with people from cultures I had learned about in library books—my true transformation started to happen when I went back to the source and repaired the connections I had severed with those first significant people in my life.

Epilogue

Fig. 22. Alvenia Bridges at the Sugar Bar. By Maya Angela Smith.

Fig. 23. Alvenia Bridges wearing a letter jacket with an inscription from Mick Jagger. By Maya Angela Smith.

This photo (Fig. 22) was from when Alvenia and I went to open mic night hosted by Valerie Simpson at the Sugar Bar. Alvenia put together a striking outfit with her signature pearls and rounded out her look with one of her stylish hats. She has a hat for every occasion and rarely leaves home without one. Ever since James Finney passed away, she has refused to allow anyone else to touch her hair, adorning her head with hats instead.

The other photo (Fig. 23) captures the time Alvenia showed me her She's
the Boss *jacket by strutting around the apartment to model it for me. I was
mesmerized by how the regality of her pearls, which never leave her neck,
contrasted with the sporty nature of what was essentially a letter jacket.
This item was not displayed for all to see. She kept it lovingly tucked away.
When she did lay eyes on it after so many years, she decided that she could
only really do it justice if she wore it. So, she took it to get dry-cleaned.
Alvenia laughed when she recollected the reaction from the cleaners. It was
much like my reaction was when I first saw it: "Wait, what?"*

*Alvenia loves this jacket because it shows what she meant to Mick. He
gave it to her on her birthday as a sign of appreciation for her hard work
on his first solo album. After I admired the stitching on the front, she shot
me a mischievous grin and let me in on a little secret. Sewn on the inside
along the length of the zipper are the words "Alvenia 1ˢᵗ 100% Club. No one
else belongs." When I asked her what it meant, she smiled coyly and said,
"It means that I'm one of a kind and I'm untouchable." Throughout her
life, she often had to fight to belong. In this case, she was the only one who
did belong. She was in charge of her own destiny and story. She mattered.*

"Alvenia, why don't we go to open mic at the Sugar Bar tomorrow
night? Just you and me? You can reminisce about when you were a
weekly staple there and then show off those dance moves that you're
always telling me about." An academic conference had brought me back
to New York in March of 2019, so I tacked on a few extra days to consult
with Alvenia on the book. She had just finished lamenting how she
missed her Thursday night jaunts to Nick Ashford and Val Simpson's
restaurant and performance space. Even though it was only a short stroll
up Broadway, Alvenia's mobility—limited by that fateful tumble down

those stairs and then exacerbated by osteoporosis—coupled with her lack of disposable income made such outings an unrealistic extravagance.

Since it opened in 1996, the Sugar Bar has been the place to go for live soul and R&B music, often attracting unknown or up-and-coming performers, such as when Alicia Keys graced the stage before she was a household name and electrified an already energetic atmosphere. Nick and Val would often perform to the delight of the patrons, since they were not only the owners but also the heart and soul of the establishment. Alvenia was curious how different it would be since Nick's passing in 2011.

"Did I ever tell you that Nick was the person who first put it in my head that I should write a memoir?" Alvenia deflected my question about returning to the Sugar Bar by doing what she always does best: answering my question with a tangentially related story:

"He had been on a plane and somehow came across that photo of me and Jerry Hall behind the giant fuzzy black ball (Fig. 8). I had never seen the photo. I didn't even know it was ever published. I learned later that Nick had seen a reprinting of a 1975 issue of *Vogue Italia*. He had taken the magazine from the plane to show me. Sounding shocked, he lovingly teased, 'I didn't know you were so well endowed, Alvenia! There's so much I don't know about you. You should write a book that tells your life story.' I wish I could tell him that his idea is finally coming to fruition."

This memory of Nick Ashford elicited a chortle from Alvenia before she launched into the reason why she stopped attending open mic night at the Sugar Bar in the first place:

"It was just too hard for me with Nick no longer there. I even almost didn't go to his funeral because I couldn't bear to say goodbye. In the end, though, I was glad I went because of how lovely it honored him. Val brought the spirit of their white parties to the memorial service. She looked resplendent in green as she regaled the crowd with hilarious stories about Nick. It was standing room only at the Abyssinian Baptist Church in Harlem and while the service had begun with tears of sorrow, it culminated in tears of laughter. Val really had us in stitches with one particular scene: one night she checked on Nick in his dressing room because he was making a lot of noise. Apparently, he couldn't figure out what to wear. As Val was giving him some suggestions, he picked up his perfume and sprayed it all over his body including his ankles. When Val inquired to why the ankles needed perfume, he said in a deadpan manner, 'You never know when someone might want to kiss my feet!' That was Nick and the spirit that he brought with him."[1]

As Alvenia sat lost in her thoughts, I figured I would try one more time: "It seems like going to his funeral allowed you to find closure. Perhaps, going back to open mic night will provide you with something you need as well. Besides, the whole evening is on me." She had been quite vocal about how her current personal issues were getting her down. I was hoping a trip to the Sugar Bar would provide a much-needed pick-me-up.

"You are right. That place has been a source of so much joy. Perhaps it's time for me to revive open mic Thursdays. Your gift means the world to me."

Once Alvenia has her mind set on something, it's impressive to watch her in action. When I informed her that the restaurant was completely booked for open mic that week, she put in a series of calls. She had

---

1. For more information, see "Thousands Gather."

once known everyone who worked there and through her connections, she was able to get us a table. Then she started to meticulously plan her evening. "I want to show you the hat I'm thinking about wearing tomorrow night. I know I can't wear fur because it's springtime and I don't want people to think that I've lost it. But I'm sure I have a suitable hat. Barbara Harris, Miss Tee, Val Simpson—these are some of the fiercest Black women in the music industry. I have to be appropriately dressed." As she said this, I started thinking that perhaps I would need to buy an outfit as well. I hadn't packed anything fancy for what was essentially a business trip. Once Alvenia started gathering other parts of her ensemble, I definitely knew some shopping was in order, even though clothes shopping was as boring to me as watching paint dry. Alvenia might not go out on the town the way she used to, but she had spent most of her adult life as a fashion icon. A few years out of the loop was not going to take away her impeccable style. Besides, everything she owned was now considered vintage and trendy.

The next evening, I tried on my new thrift store dress to Alvenia's approval. I then watched as she meticulously added various accessories to her ensemble: multiple strands of pearls around her neck with earrings to match, her stylish black hat that was apparently appropriate for the season and a deep red shade of lipstick. Finally, she chose one of her favorite walking sticks. As she had told Finney all those years earlier, "She was on the loose."

When we exited the elevator in the lobby—it was finally working again after a spate of repairs—Alvenia asked Willie, the doorman and one of her favorite people in the world, to take a photo of us. She wanted to document her attempt at reincorporating those moments of joy that had once been instrumental in getting her through some of those difficult phases of her life.

The ride to the restaurant was short but teeming with expectation. While we sat in the cab, Alvenia gushed about her excitement over seeing everyone. She had watched many members of the Sugar Bar family grow up in her years of patronage and was looking forward to reuniting with those who worked there. However, when I got out of the car and tried to help her out, she wouldn't move at first. She didn't recognize the hostess at the door and expressed anxiety that the Sugar Bar had changed and that it would no longer feel familiar. It took a few moments of my coaxing her, against the backdrop of an increasingly annoyed taxi driver, before she eventually decided to exit the vehicle. But the apprehension remained as we approached the door. Finally, I heard a woman exclaim with glee from right inside the doorway, "Ms. Alvenia. I'm so glad you could join us." At that point, Alvenia's eyes lit up, and the invisible forcefield that hadn't let her pass the threshold finally relinquished its power.

"Q, I'm so happy to see you!" she gushed. A beautiful, confident woman grabbed Alvenia's hands in hers and told the hostess that she would show us to our table. She then led us to a corner table right next to the stage and left us with some menus.

As we settled into our seats, Alvenia turned to me and remarked, "When I saw Q, it was like a dream. I kept searching for my balance as I tried to get out of the cab. It wasn't until I saw him that I found my balance. He used to ride his bike through the park and would end up at my place for snacks." As Alvenia reminisced about her history with Q, I gently interrupted to note that I had heard the hostess use the pronoun "she."

"Thank you for reminding me. It's not like he—she changed her hair. I am going to learn how to say 'she' although from force of habit, it may take me a few attempts. It is so beautiful to see her transition as a woman. She's so much more comfortable in her skin because she finally gets to be who she really is. You know, she was the one who came over to me at the white party and forced me to accept Maya and Oprah's invitation. If she hadn't literally moved the chair from under me, I might not have worked up the courage."

Then as we peered at the menu's options, another gorgeous woman came over, strutting in her high heels with a fierceness that commanded respect.

"Miss Tee!" Alvenia gasped. "Thank you for finding us a table on such a packed night."

"Alvenia, you know you are always welcome. I hope we get to start seeing you on a regular basis," she replied with a deep, silky, southern accent.

"I hope so, Miss Tee. I hope so."

Miss Tee smiled, excused herself and ran off to take care of some business. It was a big job managing this space. The musicians had just arrived and she needed to make sure they were well taken care of. Alvenia then turned to me: "When I spotted Q, I was transported back to all those evenings I spent here. She was like my anchor. Then when I saw Miss Tee, I not only saw her but all her warmth. It was that moment that I knew I was home."

After our delicious meal, the restaurant transformed itself into open mic night. The lights dimmed, the stage filled with musicians and then Valerie Simpson surrounded by the other supporting vocals, took a seat at the table next to ours. The MC introduced a night full of performers, mainly singers with the occasional comedian sprinkled in. For each song, Val and her entourage would provide a chorus of backup vocals. I had never been to an open mic quite like this. The highlight for me was when a woman requested "Ain't No Mountain High Enough." Upon hearing this, Val abruptly got out of her seat and took the stage. After politely asking the keyboardist to move, she informed the audience that since she wrote this song, she was the one who should be playing it. It was probably a good thing too because the poor singer—the worst of the evening—butchered the whole song and actually needed Val's periodic encouragement to keep going as the crowd looked on stunned. I couldn't help but feel the utmost respect for this legend as she decided to be nurturing and supportive when someone offered such a cringe-worthy rendition of her best-known song. Then, Val continued to exude warmth and generosity when she took the mic at the end of the first set to acknowledge Alvenia's presence in the audience. Alvenia beamed with pride, although I also noticed a flinch of what looked like regret. She confided later, "Coming here, it's like being reborn. My heart is pounding. For some stupid reason, I deprived myself."

As Alvenia sat there near the stage, she didn't just grab the attention of people she knew, complete strangers would also stop by to say hi. There was something that made people gravitate to Alvenia. I had always felt that centripetal force pulling me into orbit around her, but since I rarely saw her outside the apartment, I seldom got to witness her power over others. One woman in particular approached us after her turn at the mic and told Alvenia how stunning she was and that she looked like Josephine Baker. Alvenia thanked her meekly and then winked at me, "I used to hear that all the time. Wow, that was ages ago." Alvenia went on to explain how she always took being compared to Josephine Baker as the ultimate compliment.

For some reason it had never crossed my mind—perhaps because Alvenia had lived such a serendipitous and astounding life that it was hard for me to compare her to other people—but there were so many similarities between Alvenia Bridges and Josephine Baker. What struck me first was how both of them had the name Venus bestowed upon them at some point in their lives. Josephine's adoring fans dubbed her the bronze Venus, a moniker that traveled far and wide, while Alvenia cherished the name Venus because it was what John Von Neumann affectionately called her—Venus was a name they shared with each other, cloaked in the intimacy of their friendship. It was the only nickname Alvenia ever accepted. In doing so, she claimed it as a part of her and made it her own. She proudly embodied the power, grace, beauty, and love associated with Venus's mythical status.

But the similarities between Alvenia and Josephine go much deeper than a name. While Josephine was born almost forty years before Alvenia, they both were from Missouri border towns—Alvenia from Kansas City, Kansas and Josephine from St. Louis, Missouri—where they were affected by oppressive Jim Crow laws and unrelenting racism. There were also marked parallels in their family lives. Neither of them knew who their father was and spent much of their childhoods wondering what he was like. Alvenia and Josephine both also suffered tumultuous relationships with their mothers, which led them to run away and eventually end up in New York. They both were extraordinarily skinny, which was not a coveted trait at the time, but they managed to transform this disadvantage into a career. Alvenia ignored her mother's cruel taunts about her orangutan limbs, using her six-foot frame accentuated by her impressively long legs to break into the modeling world—a world that even to this day seldom acknowledges Black women's beauty. Meanwhile, although Josephine failed to secure numerous chorus line positions because she was "too thin, too small, too dark," she used her skinny limbs and comical gestures to create a memorable persona, becoming "the highest paid chorus girl in the world" and then one of the most iconic women ever to exist.[2] Importantly, it was Europe, not America, where they would first taste what it was like to be seen as human and not solely as Black women. Even though Europe had very specific and narrow ideas of how Black womanhood should be performed, Alvenia and Josephine pushed those boundaries on their own terms.

Both these women showed tenacity, creativity, and resolve to forge the lives they did, but I couldn't help but notice that they also shared the same fate of achieving and then losing the financial solvency that they had acquired against all odds. Josephine's unpaid debts caused her to lose the castle that she had bought during the height of her career, while Alvenia was barely holding on to the rent-stabilized apartment she had obtained at the height of hers. As an interesting side note, Mick Jagger attended the opening night of Josephine's comeback tour *Joséphine à Bobino 1975* in Paris, which received critical acclaim but was cut short by Josephine's death a few days later from a cerebral hemorrhage. She was found lying in bed surrounded by newspapers celebrating her triumphant return—perhaps a bittersweet ending to an enigmatic life where the protagonist comes out on top but never gets to fully enjoy

---

2. Phyllis Rose, *Jazz Cleopatra: Josephine Baker in Her Time.* 1st ed., Doubleday, 1989, p. 53, p. 11.

it. What would a comeback for Alvenia look like and who would be there to witness it?

In some ways, Alvenia was already making a comeback. She was dressed up, at one of her favorite spots, reconnecting with people who were dear to her and making waves with people she didn't know. More importantly, when the music moved her, she was on her feet. The band played some interludes between open-mic participants and when they performed a Beatles-Red Hot Chili Peppers mash up of "Come Together" and "Give it Away," she really started rocking out. Alvenia was a rocker through and through. At one point, her moves were so fluid and so energetic, I thought that we had been transported to one of those southern revival meetings where the congregants enter with all manner of infirmities, are miraculously healed and then dance their praise to the applause of all the worshippers. Alvenia's movement seemed impossible given her knee problems, but then again, dancing always took her to another world. It was similar to Saturday mornings when she would tune into 88.3 for their four hours of Motown hits. When I would happen upon her during one of these sessions, she would always draw me in and proudly proclaim that she was still a killer dancer, "Dancing is everything to me and I have no control over it whatsoever. I don't know how people enjoy themselves without it. It's freedom and it's spiritual beyond belief." Dancing alongside her, I could feel whatever this feeling was that she had described to me so many times. Moving with the Sugar Bar's energy, she was not confined to her home space, but sharing joy with the world through the activity that had allowed her to travel the world in the first place.

A little after 1:00 a.m., I informed Alvenia that we had been there for over five hours. She didn't believe me at first until I showed her my watch.

While I'm pretty sure she could've stayed another five hours, I was on my last wind and finally convinced her it was time to go home.

As we made our way to the door, Alvenia spotted Miss Tee and excitedly declared, "I'm coming back every Thursday" to which Miss Tee responded, "Well of course! What else are you going to do?" They then embraced.

Once we arrived home, we still stayed up a couple hours more as Alvenia shared with me her emotions from the evening and reiterated her vow that she would make this a usual occurrence, "The distraction of all the roommates and just holding onto my apartment has taken all my energy, but when I saw Miss Tee, I realized how I closed that door and all the beauty it added to my life. Where we were seated was where Nick and Val used to sit when they ran open mic night together. I could feel Nick's energy still with me. This is the place where I want to be."

Alvenia has since made it to the Sugar Bar a couple times. One of the most special experiences was when her friend Barbara Harris informed her of a Roberta Flack tribute that Val was hosting. Roberta was recovering from a stroke and so her friends in the industry wanted to do something special for her. For years, Alvenia has yearned to reunite with Roberta—the woman she credits with getting her into the music business and taking a chance on her when there was really no reason to. One of my fondest memories with Alvenia was back in 2014 when I was her roommate. We attended Roberta's Lincoln Center Out of Doors concert. It was there that Alvenia first shared with me some of the incredible details of her life on the road with Roberta. I had asked Alvenia if she ever tried to contact Roberta, a question that upset her more than I could've imagined. She explained how a man she described as "the Queen who Walks her Dogs" wouldn't let her near Roberta, but Alvenia couldn't provide a reason why. Relaying this fact was one of the first times Alvenia seemed visibly upset in front of me, but she quickly shook it off to enjoy being in the moment where she was surrounded by adoring fans that had accompanied Roberta for over forty years.

Years later, Alvenia was finally going to get her chance to reunite with Roberta. When she arrived at the Sugar Bar, Miss Tee escorted Alvenia right by security and seated her in the corner near where she and I spent that open mic night together. About half an hour later, Alvenia noticed security grew very tight as they made space for Roberta to maneuver her wheelchair. As she rolled by, Alvenia felt the Spirit whisper to her that this was her chance. She leapt up and planted a kiss on Roberta's cheek, much to the dismay of her entourage who quickly rolled her on stage. When Roberta realized who had touched her with so much affection, she called out Alvenia's name with elation. That was all Alvenia had ever wanted, to let Roberta know that she would always have a place in her heart. A few moments later, "the Queen who Walks her Dogs" approached Alvenia and without so much of a greeting, told her in a tone dripping with disdain, "Follow me, Alvenia." Then, as Alvenia joined Roberta backstage, Roberta looked her in the eye, smiled with all the pride that a former mentor feels when seeing her protégé after many years and said, "I think I can use your energy."

At that moment, Alvenia became covered in goosebumps so dense that they had to fight each other for room. "It was so overwhelmingly beautiful. I entered such a happy, happy place."

Alvenia had thought about this possible moment for years. What would it be like for her to reconnect with the woman who had guided her into an extremely important stage of her life? As Alvenia's sister reminded her one day on the phone, "You have to put it out there. The universe will give you what you want if you ask it." The universe had been bountiful and answered her wish, but it wasn't done providing for her yet. What Alvenia didn't know was that at the same time that she was with Roberta backstage, Howard King, Roberta's former drummer—wheelchair bound just like she was—had wheeled himself in and, under Miss Tee's direction, had taken his position next to where Alvenia had been sitting. When Alvenia returned to her seat, he threw up his arms, shouting "Fooled you!" and tenderly embraced Alvenia who at this point was bursting with joy.

Howard King was with Alvenia on her inaugural tour and got to witness Alvenia learn the ropes and prove herself as a topnotch tour manager. Roberta was the last person that Howard would play for. Nicknamed "the Locksmith" because of his even groove,[3] Howard had left the Bronx right before his high school graduation because he had been invited to join jazz saxophonist Gary Bartz on the road. He then traded in his spot to study under Max Roach at the University of Massachusetts for a chance to play at the Montreux Jazz Festival in Switzerland, a venue known for attracting people like Miles Davis, Nina Simone, Ella Fitzgerald, and B.B. King.

Howard travelled all over Europe and was soon courted by Harry Belafonte who needed a drummer who could read music, a skill that

---

3. Jimmy Heath and Joseph McLaren, *I Walked with Giants: The Autobiography of Jimmy Heath,* Temple University Press, 2010, p. 177.

most of the jazz musicians did not possess. Harry challenged him to work on a whole different level, both musically and personally. Harry not only expanded Howard's repertoire, but he also elevated his experience on the road, from the types of hotels he stayed at to the amount of money he earned. Harry was practically a diplomat and received the treatment benefitting the title. Harry prepared Howard for his crossover into more mainstream music and when Howard joined Roberta in 1979, the same year that Alvenia became tour manager, he was ready to tour with one of the most exacting performers in the music industry. Roberta suffered no fools and Alvenia was the perfect person to keep a bunch of unruly men on track.

Being under the thumb of two iron ladies was worth it, though. As Howard explained in a phone conversation with me, "For a woman, Alvenia had a lot of balls and I mean that with all due respect." He was able to blossom as a performer and a person by playing fancy concert halls instead of seedy clubs. Furthermore, he learned the importance of being on time for rehearsals and gigs, he acquired strategies for better handling his money such as when he signed a contract with Alvenia that forbade her to administer his per diem while they were playing in Vegas and he experienced the incredible feeling of hearing himself on the radio.

The latter is a gift that he still cherishes. On any given day he might feel horrible about where he ended up in life, but if he hears himself in a song on the radio, it brings him up, gives him space to breathe and reminds him that things aren't that bad. Since the early eighties, when a car accident left him in a coma and then paraplegic, he has relied on those chance encounters with himself on the radio as moral support. The reminder of how "he used to be somebody," as he puts it, is what allows him to trudge forward.

When I asked Howard what it was like to see Roberta after all those years, he admitted feeling an overwhelming sadness. He knew what it was like to be disoriented from a stroke because he had similar difficulties when coming out of his coma. He understood the look she gave him—a look where she knew she should recognize him but just couldn't—because he suffered his own battles with overstimulation as he recovered. It was a frustrating place to be. The fact that Roberta did not recognize him put into further relief just how special the moment that Alvenia had shared with Roberta was.

Alvenia and Howard got to catch up at Roberta's tribute amidst all the people that had been a part of her musical career at some point or another. They reminisced about the year they worked together. Howard would later tell me during our interview, "When we were on the road, we had no idea that this was Alvenia's first gig. I didn't believe it. Roberta was her training. Alvenia did her homework and learned fast. I could depend on what she said. And being on the road with a bunch of guys was a monumental task. She was all business."

Thinking about how Alvenia related to me the story of Mick Jagger calling her untouchable and Bill Graham telling her that she was *bad*, I asked Howard to give me a sense of what she was like on the road. He described how effective she was at being a chameleon. She was a master at knowing what a situation dictated and embodying the qualities that she needed to succeed:

"I remember how she was in jeans for our first gig. But when we got overseas and got into her element, she transformed into a whole other person. I think she's a little more continental at heart. She was more put together and classy than we were. We were more bohemian, jazzy, and from the streets. But she interacted with us very well and was able to maintain a certain respectable distance without making people feel uncomfortable. And while some men had a problem with women in authority, she was very diplomatic about it and could always get them to bend her way."

He then added with a chuckle, "My traumatic brain injury has affected my balance, my memory, and my speech, but I will never forget the moment she went down to the hotel pool in her bikini. She cleans up well."

While Marty Klein had been so sure that Alvenia would fail miserably on the road and eventually go crawling on her knees back to Seventh Avenue, because he saw her as nothing more than some two-bit model who was deluded to think she could play with the big boys, Alvenia had used the poise and gumption that had gotten her through the trials of her childhood and the wanderings of her twenties and thirties to craft a career that pretty much stunned everyone around her. And she did so while staying true to herself and her character. As someone who yearned for guidance throughout her early years, she used her inner voice and the opportunities that key figures offered her throughout her life to create her own path and direction.

In February 2020, Alvenia's musical past came knocking at her door again when her former colleague, Jerry Pompili from Bill Graham Presents, contacted her to invite her to the opening of the Bill Graham and the Rock and Roll Revolution exhibit at the New York Historical

Society.[4] They wanted her to be a guest of honor. Alvenia had been thinking about Bill a lot recently. The news of Kobe Bryant's helicopter crash had just rocked the world. For Alvenia, it was eerily similar to the moment she had found out about Bill Graham's crash thirty years prior.

Three thousand miles away from the wreckage—news travels so fast these days—Alvenia looked at the photo of Bill, hanging where it had been for thirty years, and sighed. "The tower had told him no." Bill just looked back at her, shrugging. This was the way of things. Steve Kahn and Ara Zobayan were the best pilots in the business. If anyone could fly in inclement weather, they could. They had both been cleared to fly. They had been advised not to. But they had been allowed to. Was it ever worth the risk?

When I called Alvenia to check on how she was taking the news of Kobe's death, she explained her philosophy to me, "The Spirit is asking: what do I have to do to shake things up and make people love each other again? But what I really want to know is how does the Spirit decide who it sacrifices?" She may have started by talking about Kobe and the others, but she landed on Bill, as she always does. After three decades, Bill Graham's death still occupies an outsized space in Alvenia's memory. He was someone who had changed the world, her world. Bill was more than the godfather of the rock concert. He was the person who allowed her to reach her full potential and she owed much of her self-discovery to him. As such, she was looking forward to honoring his memory by attending the Rock and Roll Revolution event.

---

4. Exhibition highlights can be found here: https://www.nyhistory.org/exhibitions/bill-gra ham-rock-and-roll-revolution.

However, preparations for the event weren't going as planned. She had been expecting an invitation by mail, an invitation that never came. Jerry called her to inquire how things were going with her RSVP. When she explained that she hadn't received her invitation, he provided her a number to call to put herself on the guest list. At that point, Alvenia told him that that was not how things were done in this business. Jerry assured her that a guestlist was normal procedure, but she refused to accept his answer. "That's not how things are done. That's not protocol," she kept repeating to me, when I tried as well to convince her that times had changed and RSVPing without an invitation was more common these days. She understood what I said in theory but reminded me that she works by a certain code and is going to stick to that code. Besides, how would she know what to wear without an invitation indicating the proper attire? I argued that people weren't as concerned about dress codes these days, but she responded that she's not *people*. This is true. Alvenia has always been a woman apart.

After our conversation meandered to other topics, I circled back around to try one last time because I knew how important this opportunity was to her. But she articulated that she wasn't going to show up to a lavish affair teeming with media and fancy guests, so that they could witness her embarrassment when she was denied entry at the door. She wouldn't be able to take the rejection. At that moment, I flashed on all the strategies she had devised throughout her life to claim space in places not meant for her, places often openly hostile to her presence. She had been told numerous times in her life that she didn't belong. She learned to stake a claim by following protocol and arming herself with proof. Proof, such as a tangible, paper invitation in hand. That's why her work contracts were always so important to her and why she would follow them to the tee. When she knew what she needed to do and had proof in what she was doing, no one could tell her otherwise. It all made so much sense now.

Even though I hadn't heard Alvenia this excited in years, she was ready to sacrifice this chance to reunite with her former colleagues and to experience the energy of this public memorialization of Bill simply because she didn't trust the system to protect her and she was too old to deal with yet more marginalization. Alvenia's predicament was heartbreaking for me. The cracks in her voice broadcast the utter distress she was feeling. All I could say to her was that I hoped things would work out.

The next day I felt an overwhelming urge to interfere in the whole affair. I'm not the meddling type and wasn't sure if Alvenia would appreciate my jumping into the fray, but this opportunity was too important to let slip away without a fight. I found Jerry Pompili's number through a simple internet search and decided to call him and see if we could figure out a solution that would satisfy everyone. As the line picked up, I encountered a chipper message from his home answering machine informing me that I had reached the Pompilis. I barely realized home landlines still existed and panicked since I didn't have a message ready. I am embarrassed to admit that I hung up abruptly, vowing to call back in a little while when I had a chance to come up with an adequate explanation for why a complete stranger was calling him.

A few minutes later, I received a call from a San Rafael number that looked familiar. Turned out he was calling back to inquire about the missed call. I explained to him somewhat sheepishly that I was a friend of Alvenia's and that I had called to try to figure out something that would allow Alvenia to go to the Bill Graham exhibit because I knew she wanted to attend more than anything. He was much more accommodating than

I expected and told me he would call me back. A few minutes later, he was true to his word. He had gotten in touch with Alvenia's close friend Michael, who would take it upon himself to make sure Alvenia attended the event. I thanked Jerry profusely and asked him not to mention to Alvenia that I had called. I wasn't yet ready to admit my meddling to her.

The days leading up to the event, I called Alvenia a few times to see how logistics were coming along for the opening. She told me that something might be in the works, but she wasn't very forthcoming. I realized I would just have to be patient and find out after the fact. A couple days after the event, Alvenia called with a tinge to her voice I hadn't heard in years. It was laden with happiness. She managed to attend the opening with Michael, who she affectionately called the Secretary—an inside joke decades old. The Secretary had told her to expect him in her lobby at five p.m. She arrived at 4:15 and waited the forty-five minutes in anticipation. As she reminded me, she always arrives early. Willie, the doorman, set up a seat for her near him so she could be comfortable and would have someone to chat with to help calm her nerves. He could see what a basket case she had become. She had been dreaming of this night for a month, ever since Jerry had sent her the press release of the event.

While she waited in the lobby, two of her neighbors asked to take a picture with her because they were blown away by her glamour. She assured me that she wasn't wearing anything that special. Just something that she described as "just me"—an all-black outfit with a cool little hat. When I asked Alvenia why she stood out to her neighbors that evening, she replied, "I just had my attitude. They knew I meant business." She then added coyly, "Besides, I have to say that I looked pretty alright." Having gone out on the town with Alvenia before, I knew that "pretty alright" was an understatement.

The Secretary arrived at five p.m. on the dot and escorted Alvenia to the Historical Society. As they exited the cab, he told her to wait for him on the steps while he acquired their passes. The event was swarming with expectant people since the exhibition had already been a success on the West Coast and because Bill's short-lived Fillmore East venue was an important episode in New York rock and roll history. Just as the Secretary returned with passes, Alvenia looked up and saw Jerry walking quickly toward her. They hadn't seen each other in thirty years, but according to her, it couldn't have been too difficult to spot her in the crowd. Not many of the patrons looked like her. Years later, she still sticks out wherever she goes.

Jerry approached her, beaming with satisfaction. "You made it!" he exclaimed before embracing her warmly and excusing himself to return to the stage. Jerry had been the number one employee at Bill Graham Presents. He and three other original employees were about to participate in an on-stage walk down memory lane as they talked about how it all began in the sixties. Alvenia was in awe to hear all the history, much of which she didn't know.

Then David Graham, Bill's son, joined the stage. Alvenia was taken aback by the fact that he was a grown, middle-aged man. Alvenia hadn't seen him since his twenty-first birthday party, which had been a major step in father and son's reconciliation, a reconciliation that was tragically cut short because of Bill's untimely death a few weeks after. Alvenia reminded me how she had been in charge of logistics for that birthday. It was something she talked about often.

Afterwards, the Secretary led them to the exhibit itself. Using special headsets, they embarked on a whole adventure of Bill's life. While enjoying the experience immensely, the exhibit was too crowded to navigate.

He told Alvenia they should return on a more mellow day and go to dinner instead. That's when he took her to one of her favorite restaurants, Trattoria del Arte, whose waitstaff still remembered her even though she hadn't dined there in years. She had been such a regular back in the day that they had given her a plaque years ago. All the servers kept asking her where she had been. Just like with the Sugar Bar, she was touched by the reception but also had to manage small pangs of sadness for no longer having access to all the haunts of her youth.

Alvenia returned home around 9 p.m. and Willie was waiting for her when she entered the lobby.

"You're back from heaven?" he ventured as she greeted him with a Cheshire smile. The evening had been a dream come true, one of the most extraordinary experiences of her life. She explained to Willie how she was able to pay homage to the man who changed her life, "The whole experience was over the moon." She then retreated to her apartment and gleefully left a voicemail on Jerry's machine, even though he wouldn't be returning to California for several days, to thank him from the bottom of her heart.

As she relayed this story to me, she stopped for a second and then thought out loud, "Something doesn't make sense with all of this. How did the Secretary know to reach out to me? If he hadn't, I don't think I would've ever made it there." At this point, I decided to come clean. I told her that I hoped she wouldn't be mad for meddling in her business and then confessed how I had contacted Jerry and begged him to find a way to make sure she could attend the event.

"I can't believe that all this time, I was telling you my story and in reality, it was your story. You created this. This is too mucking fuch—that's a Finneyism—too mucking fuch." We both laughed because we knew how much she loved peppering her stories with Finneyisms. Her dear departed friend James Finney had a way with words like none other. But then she became serious as she solemnly said to me:

"Meddling in my business? You weren't meddling in my business. You were meddling with my life and death. That wasn't a Valentine's present. That wasn't even a birthday present. That was a life present. I had been thinking that if I couldn't get in to see Bill, something was wrong with me. It would mean that I was no longer the person I once was. I was no longer Alvenia."

At this point, I breathed a sigh of relief. All I had ever wanted was for her to feel like herself. As I was about to respond, Alvenia continued expressing her gratitude:

"This is going to sound corny, but I sat with Bill's photo after the opening and told him that things are going to change because of the book, our memoir. And today, when I woke up, I got all the energy back that I thought I didn't have any more. I've been thanking the Spirit all day and now I realize that it was you! When I saw all those people there to celebrate Bill's life and influence on the music industry, I could feel his energy all through the joint. I was floating around that night. I just knew that the Spirit had something to do with this and was reminded of my blessings, reminded that nobody can take my joy. Thank you for helping me get my strength back. I feel alive and for once I don't feel threatened by the system. I keep peptalking to myself about this and how I'm gonna come through, gonna come through, gonna come through all the things that are weighing me down: my knee, my apartment, my financial situation etc. Because of what you did for me, I feel so much faith and that faith gives me strength. That's the Spirit. The Spirit was riding on you."

After I hung up, I kept thinking about this unnamed character in Alvenia's story, the presence that she simply calls the Spirit. She credits it with guiding her through her darkest days, first showing up in childhood when she saw no path forward other than imprisonment or death. It was the Spirit that let her know another path was possible. From flowing through her each time she danced, to creating the possibility of being on the road with some of the biggest names in the music industry, the Spirit led her to where she needed to be. Because she put her entire faith in this entity, she was able to move beyond the constraints imposed on her by a volatile immediate family and an oppressive society.

Each time she looks at the collection of memories displayed on her walls, she remembers just how far the Spirit has allowed her to travel. These memories also remind her how unique her life is—or what to many would seem like many lives. I am honored that she has entrusted me with sharing her journey, one of resolve, serendipity, foresight, and an uncanny ability to survive, to exist boldly, and to leave her mark. By giving the world her memoir, she reclaims who she is and the stories she tells. In doing so, she dares others to dream of not only seeing the world but of living in it on their own terms.

Acknowledgements

We would like to thank the many people who made this book possible. While the research and writing began in 2014, many decades of experiences are woven through the fabric of these pages. Alvenia would like to thank all the people who believed in her dreams of traveling the world. She is particularly grateful to her brother Robert, who knew he had the right to be a person of color and the world's ignorance couldn't stop him; Mama Beatrice, who gave Alvenia that globe and radio and purchased her plane ticket out of Kansas; John Von Neumann, who made seeing multiple corners of the world possible for her; James Finney, who was a guiding light from Los Angeles to New York and beyond; Jimi Hendrix, whose brief encounter showed her that there are messengers among us; Roberta Flack, who saw Alvenia's potential and paved her way into show business; Mick Jagger, who gave her a chance to truly soar; and Bill Graham, whose respect allowed her to better believe in herself.

Maya is indebted to her amazing family members who have supported her writing journeys no matter where they lead: her parents Emily and Elton Smith and her brother Jonathan Smith, who instilled curiosity and a love of storytelling; her husband Rohit Eipe, who is an amazing thought partner and supporter; and her son Amar'e who constantly pushes her to see the world differently. Maya is grateful to her colleagues at the University of Washington and other places, who have provided feedback, brainstormed concepts, lent moral support, served as beta readers, and helped with digital humanities projects related to the book. In particular, she expresses gratitude to Anne Liu Kellor, Norea Hoeft,

Verletta Kern, Hayley Park, Maryam Fakouri, Oliver Gordon, Nithin Coca, Livi Yoshioka-Maxwell, Alina Tonu, Nicole Butts, Jessica Blois, Maureen Devlin, Kathy Liddle, Rick Kern, Maureen Mahon, Francesca Royster, Eric Weisbard, and members of the Popular Music Books in Process series.

Alvenia and Maya would both like to thank their agent Mariah Nichols, who offered representation the day before Maya gave birth to her son (talk about timing, and perhaps a metaphor for the publishing process). Mariah was an early believer in the book and offered insightful feedback to get the manuscript ready for submission. They would also like to thank everyone at Rising Action Publishing Collective, especially Alexandria Brown and Tina Beier, for creating an amazing press for new authors. The support and care they provide is a model for the industry.

Last but not least, Alvenia and Maya want to profusely thank Anthony Giordano, without whom this book might not have ever crossed the finish line. With Alvenia and Maya living almost 3,000 miles apart, Anthony served as the glue that allowed the partnership to thrive in long distance. They are forever indebted to his myriad skills and his huge heart.

About the Authors

Alvenia Bridges is an American author with a life story full of intrigue, serendipity, courage, and resolve. From humble beginnings in Kansas, she managed to travel the world and make a name for herself by supporting some of the biggest figures in the music industry such as Roberta Flack, Mick Jagger, and Bill Graham. She currently lives in New York City. Reclaiming Venus is her first memoir.

Maya Angela Smith is an American author who writes about language, race, migration, music, and identity. Her first book, *Senegal Abroad*, won the Modern Language Association's French and Francophone Studies Award. She lives in Seattle where she is a Professor in the French and Italian Studies department at the University of Washington. She is also a visual artist who has shown her work in Paris, New York, Houston, the Bay Area, and Seattle. Reclaiming Venus is her first memoir. Her upcoming book, *Ne me quitte pas*, will be published in early 2025 with Duke University Press.

Bibliography

Angelou, Maya. *I Know Why the Caged Bird Sings,* Random House, 1970.

Angelou, Maya. *Letter to My Daughter*, 1st ed., Random House, 2008.

Angelou, Maya. *Mom & Me & Mom*. Random House, 2013.

"Bill Graham and the Rock and Roll Revolution." *New York Historical Society*. . Accessed February 26, 2023.

"Bill Graham Biography." *Bill Graham Memorial Foundation*. . Accessed July 18, 2019.

Covo di Nord-Est. . Accessed July 18, 2019.

Crowhurst, Anna-Marie. "Forgotten Women: The Taboo-Smashing Queen of Funk." *Stylist*, 2019. . Accessed July 18, 2019.

Garson, Helen S. *Oprah Winfrey: A biography*. Greenwood, 2004.

German, Bill. *Under their Thumb: How a Nice Boy from Brooklyn Got Mixed Up with the Rolling Stones*. Villard, 2009.

Guétary, Hélène. Accessed February 26, 2023.

Heath, Jimmy, and McLaren, Joseph. *I Walked with Giants: The Autobiography of Jimmy Heath,* Temple University Press, 2010.

Hendrix, Janie L. and McDermott, John. *Jimi Hendrix: An Illustrated Experience*. Atria, 2007.

"Hugh Masekela in conversation with Stewart Levine." *Design Indaba*. 2011.. Accessed July 18, 2019.

I Rolling Stones in Italia. Arnoldo Mondadori Editore, 1982.

Jones, Graham. "Live Aid 1985: A Day of Magic." *CNN*. July 6, 2005. Accessed July 18, 2019.

Jones, Robert. *I Beat Dyslexia: So Can You*. Jzk Publishing, 2000.

"July 4 Rock Concert for Peace Set for Moscow, Promoter Says." *Associated Press*, June 24, 1987. Accessed July 18, 2019.

Labelle, Patti, Randolph, Laura. *Don't Block the Blessings: Revelations of a Lifetime*. G. K. Hall, 1997.

"L'Altra Dolce Vita." *Il Giornale*. April 12, 2014. Accessed July 18, 2019.

Lambert, Bruce. "Bill Graham, Rock Impresario, Dies at 60 in Crash." *New York Times*. October 27, 1991.

Lopez, Antonio and Hemphill, Christopher. *Antonio's Girls*. Thames & Hudson, 1982.

"Making the (Steve Paul) Scene." *It's All the Streets You Crossed Not Long Ago*. June 07, 2005. Accessed July 18, 2019.

Martin, Douglas. "Steve Paul Dies at 71; Owned '60s Club in New York." *New York Times*. October 23, 2012. Accessed July 18, 2019.

McShane, Nelson. "Nelson Mandela Embraced New York City During Three-day Visit in 1990. *New York Daily News*. December 08, 2013. Accessed July 18, 2019.

Murray, James Briggs. "An interview with James Finney." *Schomburg Center for Research in Black Culture*, 1986.

Nathan, David. "Publicist Barbara Harris – A Class of Her Own." *Routes: A Guide to African-American Culture*. April 2021. Accessed February 26, 2023.

Nerlino, Joanne. "The Visual Art of Miles Davis." *The International Review of African American Art*, Summer 1997, 48-42.

Pietrowicz, Walter. "John Von Neumann--Remembering a Sports Car Pioneer." *September 8th*. 2003. Accessed July 18, 2019.

Patton, Alli. "Balloons, Blitzkriegs, and the Berlin Wall—The Meaning Behind Nena's '99 Luftballons.'" *American Songwriter*, 2022. Accessed February 26, 2023.

PBS. "Roberta Flack." *American Masters*, season 37, episode 1, 2023.

Rose, Phyllis. *Jazz Cleopatra: Josephine Baker in Her Time*. 1st ed., Doubleday, 1989.

Scavullo, Francesco. *Scavullo: Francesco Scavullo Photographs 1948-1984*. Harper & Row, 1984.

Schiro, Anne-Marie. "Fabrice Simon, 47, Designer of Glittery Evening Clothes. *New York Times*, August 5, 1998.

Schlagenhauf, Wes. "Cocaine, Boats, and Backgammon: The Insane Life of Rocky Aoki, Benihana's Founder." *Hustle*. May 02, 2018. Accessed July 18, 2019.

Segell, Michael. "Studio 54: Steve Rubell's Disco Disneyland." *Rolling Stone*. April 19, 1979. Accessed July 18, 2019.

Seymour, Craig. *Luther: The Life and Longing of Luther Vandross*. Harper Entertainment, 2004.

Shapiro, Harry and Glebbeek, Caesar. *Jimi Hendrix: Electric Gypsy*. St. Martin's Press, 1995.

Talley, André Leon. "Down South." *Vogue*. July 16, 2009. Accessed July 18, 2019.

"Thousands Gather to Bid Soul Legend Nick Ashford Farewell." *Amsterdam News*, August 31, 2011. Accessed July 18, 2019.

Turner, Tina. *My Love Story*. Atria Books, 2018.

Weber, Jonathan. "Bay Area Plays Tribute to Graham." *Los Angeles Times*, November 04, 1991.

"'Why Kansas?' Asks an Editor." *Topeka Capital*. December 20, 1953. Accessed July 18, 2019.